POLICY AND METHODS IN GERMAN AND AMERICAN ANTITRUST LAW

POLICY AND METHODS IN GERMAN AND AMERICAN ANTITRUST LAW

A Comparative Study

James Maxeiner

PRAEGER

PRAEGER SPECIAL STUDIES • PRAEGER SCIENTIFIC

New York • Westport, Connecticut • London

Library of Congress Cataloging-in-Publication Data

Maxeiner, James.
Policy and methods in German and American antitrust law.

"Praeger special studies. Praeger scientific."
Bibliography: p.
Includes index.
1. Antitrust Law – United States. 2. Restraint of trade – United States. 3. Antitrust Law – Germany (West) 4. Restraint of trade – Germany (West) I. Title.
K3856.M38 1986 343′.072 86-8108
ISBN 0-275-92113-1 (alk. paper) 342.372

Library of Congress Catalog Card Number: 86-8108
ISBN: 0-275-92113-1

First published in 1986

Praeger Publishers, 521 Fifth Avenue, New York, NY 10175
A division of Greenwood Press, Inc.

Printed in the United States of America

The paper used in this book complies with the Permanent Paper Standard issued by the National Information Standards Organization (Z39.48-1984).

10 9 8 7 6 5 4 3 2 1

"Das Gesetz ist der Freund des Schwachen."

Schiller, *Die Braut von Messina*

Table of Contents

Foreword

A German version of this book, "Rechtspolitik und Methoden im deutschen und amerikanischen Kartellrecht: eine vergleichende Betrachtung," was accepted by the Ludwig-Maximilians-Universität München (University of Munich, Federal Republic of Germany) as a dissertation in partial fulfillment of the requirements for the degree Dr. Juris and was published by Verlag V. Florentz GmbH, Munich.

The idea for this book originated in 1979 when I was a trial attorney with the Antitrust Division of the Department of Justice and a member of the staff of the National Commission for Review of Antitrust Laws and Procedures. At that time, Professor Eberhard Günther, one of the drafters of Federal Republic of Germany's cartel law and the first president of its Federal Cartel Authority (1958 to 1976), came to Washington to hold seminars on German and European cartel law. In those seminars, Professor Günther awakened and fostered my interest in German cartel law.

The Alexander von Humboldt Foundation of Bonn, which awarded me a fellowship in memory of Max Rheinstein, and the Max Planck Institute for Foreign and International Patent, Copyright and Competition Law provided me with the resources for two years of research and study in Munich under near ideal conditions.

Academic advisor for my book was Professor Wolfgang Fikentscher, whose thorough knowledge of not only German law and methods, but also of their American counterparts, made him the ideal guide to carry out this comparative study.

I would like to thank Professors Günther and Fikentscher for their guidance and support.

I would also like to thank the many other people who helped me with this book, including: my colleagues and friends at the Max Planck Institute, the Humboldt Foundation, the Ludwig-Maximilians-Universität, and elsewhere, who gave me assistance and encouragement; Walter, Conston & Schurtman, P.C. and its staff, who provided technical support in preparing my manuscript for publication; and, my parents, Philip and Elaine Maxeiner, and my wife, Andrea Bessac Maxeiner, who through all these many years never tired of supporting my comparative studies of law.

James R. Maxeiner

Note on Terminology

Discussing two different legal systems, which employ two different languages, creates terminology problems. In this book, *German*, in references to the time after 1948, refers only to the Federal Republic of Germany ("West Germany"). *American* refers only to the United States of America. *Cartel law* is an alternative expression for German antitrust law in line with German usage (*Kartellrecht*). Finally, *he*, unless the context indicates otherwise, includes the female gender.

1

Introduction

A remarkable reversal in popular satisfaction with antitrust law has occurred: Germany – once the classic land of cartels – now enforces an antitrust law vigorously and subject to little meaningful opposition, while the United States – itself the home of antitrust law – enforces its antitrust law erratically and against significant criticism.

A generation ago such a turnabout would hardly have been anticipated. Then, the United States, its key policy planners convinced that cartelization and concentration in German industry had contributed to Nazi aggression,[1] imposed a decartelization law in occupied Germany.[2] Later, as the price for termination of its occupation, the United States compelled the Federal Republic of Germany to adopt a law against trade restraints (the *Gesetz gegen Wettbewerbsbeschränkungen* or "GWB") or simply the cartel law.[3]

German business greeted the new GWB with distrust. Yet, despite such "unfavorable beginnings," a generation later, "[i]n the classic land of cartels a free market consciousness has arisen" (former Minister for Economics Otto Graf Lambsdorff).[4] Indeed, in marking the twenty-fifth anniversary of the GWB, one leading German newspaper could even editorialize that "almost all experts judge the serviceableness of the German cartel law favorably."[5]

No similar American newspaper could reach a comparable conclusion about public acceptance of American antitrust law today. Indeed, quite the opposite is reported. One respected publication states that "[o]pposition to the nation's 90 year-old antitrust policies is beginning to sweep the country."[6] Another quotes a resigning head of one antitrust enforcement authority as having charged that parts of American antitrust law rest on "wacko economic propositions."[7]

Whatever may be the precise measure of support in each country for antitrust laws, even the most cursory observation discloses a criticism of antitrust law in the United States not matched in kind or degree in the Federal Republic. This work investigates aspects of one of the many possible explanations – legal, social, and economic – for this remarkable turnaround. It considers perhaps the most obvious question: How do the two antitrust laws differ? In partial answer it suggests that certain principal criticisms of American antitrust law reflect dissatisfaction as much with the legal methods by which that law is applied as with the material law itself. German cartel law utilizes different legal methods which avoid or mitigate many of the problems encountered in American antitrust law. That may be why comparable criticisms of German cartel law have not been made.

PRINCIPAL CRITICISMS OF AMERICAN ANTITRUST LAW

Two of the most frequently repeated criticisms of American antitrust law are that it is hopelessly uncertain and that the proceedings by which it is applied are extraordinarily drawn out and expensive. Counterparts of these criticisms are charges that when antitrust does achieve certainty or speed, it does so at the cost of economic oversimplification.

These criticisms reflect real costs encountered in American antitrust law. Uncertain economic law makes planning difficult and distorts desirable economic activity. Clumsy court procedures cause enormous litigation expenses and often delay final legal decisions until relevancy has been lost. Yet the decision which is simplified for clarity or speed may be bad as economic policy, or unfair as justice, or both. These costs have contributed to a questioning of antitrust law's compliance with the internal requirements of law, expressed in what is called the Rule of Law, and an undermining of confidence in antitrust law's usefulness as economic policy.

Why is antitrust law in the United States so uncertain? Why is it so hard to apply? Clearly both of these questions concern as much the legal methods by which antitrust law is applied as they do the material law itself.

Broadly posed, a question of legal methods arises whenever one asks how to relate an abstract legal idea to a factual situation in order to decide a concrete case.[8] In American antitrust law, it is often impossible to state the law, even in a general way useful to deciding a concrete case. One often cannot state the manner in which a legal precept is to be applied to a factual situation. These difficulties suggest that at least some of the United States' problems with antitrust law may be problems of legal methods.

There is little recognition in the United States of the role of methods in antitrust law. While doubts about the suitability of present methods are occasionally expressed, they are seldom pursued. The problems of relating the law to the concrete case are left to be treated as problems of the substantive or of the procedural law. As a result, problems of antitrust law are often accepted as necessary evils incapable of solution. Critics may acknowledge that the substantive law of antitrust could be made more certain, predictable, and easily applied, but they anticipate that the cost of such improvements must be bad economic policy. They may assume that there is a necessary trade-off between legal certainty and sophistication in handling the individual case: a mandatory choice between a per se rule and a rule of reason. Or they may recognize that antitrust procedures might be more efficient and economically sophisticated, but then assume that other values of the procedure must be sacrificed to obtain efficiency and economic sophistication.[9] Yet there is little inquiry whether the assumptions and values of the procedures are relevant in antitrust decisions or whether antitrust decisions could be made by modified procedures which would not sacrifice these values. Lack of awareness of methods thus leads to frustration: many believe that improvements in antitrust law must be "bought" at the cost of other values protected by the legal system. Accordingly, it is hardly surprising that critics who do identify methods problems are apt to invoke these problems more to argue for curtailment of antitrust law than to justify modification of the methods themselves. Resignation sets in: the legal method used in antitrust does not work well, therefore law cannot work well in antitrust.[10]

THE DIFFERENT GOALS OF COMPARATIVE LAW AND THEIR SIGNIFICANCE FOR THIS WORK

Comparison of law has many uses. Similarities between legal systems may be examined to find a common core of shared legal ideas. Differences may be investigated to find out what political or historical factors have shaped legal solutions. Comparison may be used for purely explanatory purposes, for example, when used as part of a sociology of law. Or it may have more immediate practical purposes, for example, when used in unification of law and in drafting of treaties. One of the oldest uses of comparative law is particularly practical: the study of foreign solutions to legal problems to bring critical perspective to one's own law to help in its improvement. While the foreign solution may be studied to consider its transplantation home, this use of comparative law does not require that transplantation be the object of study. Critical examination of different legal solutions heightens awareness of the problems and of the variety of solutions, and thus widens the range of potential solutions even where transplantation is not anticipated.

In this work, comparison of law provides the perspective from which to consider the continuing problems of antitrust law in the United States. Such a comparison has an immediate practical utility in that it can suggest possible solutions for American antitrust law. It can also have importance for German antitrust law, in that it can help identify strengths and weaknesses in German law. Moreover, it can help later comparisons of German and American antitrust law better adjust for differences rooted more in method than in material law.

In the past, comparison of law has tended to concentrate on comparison of specific solutions to problems of substantive law. Comparison of procedure is a relatively new development and comparison of methods is newer still.[11] The novelty suggests a certain caution. This work focuses on the role of methods in antitrust law. Are there special requirements for such a comparison?

Comparison requires comparability. This is surely no less true of comparison of legal methods than of other comparisons. In comparison of law it has become common to adopt a problem approach in order to avoid comparison of institutions which may not really be comparable. Comparison is facilitated when there is as much similarity other than the solution to the problem as possible. Then it is more likely that differences in the solution may account for different results in handling the problem. Some of the characteristics that the German and American legal systems and economies share which facilitate comparison are readily apparent. Thanks in part to the forced reception of American antitrust law, as well as to subsequent attention in the Federal Republic of Germany to American developments, German cartel law is close in substance to American antitrust law, despite significant differences in methods. Moreover the German economy, with its emphasis on competition and the wide markets open to it, is probably as similar to the U.S. economy as might be hoped. Finally, the German legal system places great emphasis on those values protected by the Rule of Law.

German history makes the Federal Republic of Germany an especially good subject for comparison with reference to the problems encountered in antitrust law in the United States. German law has long placed great emphasis on the legal certainty interest of the Rule of Law. The trauma of the Nazi dictatorship led to still greater emphasis on the Rule of Law. Germany was also once the classic land of cartels. The Nazi dictatorship used forced cartelization to control the economy. In the years since 1945, a centrally directed economic system, on the Soviet model and under Soviet compulsion, has been erected in East Germany. Germans are acutely aware of alternatives, both to the Rule of Law and to competition. If there is a necessary trade-off between wise antitrust policy and the values of the Rule of Law, it should surface in Germany.

THE DIFFERENT METHODS OF ANTITRUST LAW IN GERMANY AND IN THE UNITED STATES

The most important differences in legal methods between German cartel law and American antitrust law can be grouped into four broad categories:

1. American antitrust law is applied as a matter of judicial justice; American antitrust decisions determine rights and duties. German cartel law, on the other hand, is only sometimes applied as a matter of judicial justice. Other times, it is applied as a matter of administrative law. German cartel law decisions determine rights and duties only sometimes; other times they decide what rights and duties will be.
2. German cartel law states the law in a statute and seeks to attain a specific norm. American antitrust law relies on judge-made law found in judicial precedents deciding particular cases and does not insist on attaining a norm.
3. German cartel law is applied through subsumption of a particular factual situation under a given norm by an active decision maker. American antitrust law is applied in the resolution of a particular antitrust issue by a passive decision maker.
4. German cartel law employs centralized and specialized decision makers. American antitrust law relies on autonomous and unspecialized decision makers.

Of these differences, the last three are typical of differences between American and German legal methods generally or can be seen to be results of the German decision to apply cartel law as a mixture of adjudication and administration. That there is widespread dissatisfaction with antitrust law in the United States but not in Germany might be explained simply as dissatisfaction with American legal methods generally. The methods of the common law which prevail in the United States may be less suited to governing a highly industrialized society. On the other hand dissatisfaction with antitrust law in the United States seems greater than dissatisfaction with other areas of American law which also rely primarily on common law methods. Consequently, an explanation should be sought which would also clarify why there seems more dissatisfaction with antitrust law than with other fields of law. It thus makes sense first to turn attention to that difference between German and American methods which is not typical of differences between the respective legal systems, but which is peculiar to antitrust. That difference is that antitrust law is applied as judicial justice in the United States, but as a mixture of judicial justice and administrative law in Germany.

Although the exact lines between adjudication and administration are not clear in either the Federal Republic of Germany or in the United States, nevertheless the centers of gravity of the two are viewed similarly in both countries. Adjudication finds its center of gravity in the determination of rights and duties. Administration, on the other hand, finds its center of gravity in deciding what future legal relations will be, frequently on the basis of a discretionary decision about public welfare.[12]

That the United States opted for a judicial justice implementation of antitrust law when it adopted the Sherman Act in 1890 is not surprising. In 1890 the United States had a largely undeveloped administrative law; even today, American administrative law is considerably less developed than that of many continental countries. Moreover, throughout the formative era of antitrust law from 1890 to 1914 the dominant American view of law saw the proper role of law strictly as judicial determination of rights.[13] Finally, the drafters of the Sherman Act sought to couple their law to common law traditions regulating unreasonable restraints of trade.

Why did the Federal Republic of Germany adopt a mixed administrative and judicial system when it enacted its cartel law, the GWB, in 1957? A choice of administration was open. Thanks to the work of Otto Mayer at the turn of this century, the Federal Republic had a highly developed system of administrative law which was patterned on

French models and provided many protections against the administration.[14] To understand why the Federal Republic adopted a mixed approach, it is useful to look to the origins of German cartel law. Although the political impetus for the law came from the American occupation, the intellectual origins of the law were domestic.[15] While the drafters of the German law looked to experiences in the United States, they could find theory at home. In the years before the end of the war, a school of competition advocates arose in Germany, which was known variously as the neoliberal, Freiburg, or ORDO school. The neoliberal position had and continues to have a major role in shaping German cartel law.[16]

The neoliberals see a close connection between economy and law as elements of societal control. Organization of the economy is not value neutral. They prefer a competitive economic system not only because they consider it more efficient, but, perhaps still more important, because they believe it more democratic. They criticize purely economic perspectives that separate economic well-being from the issue of freedom.[17] They reject a centrally administered economy not only because they perceive it to be economically inefficient, but also because they consider the concentration of power in the hands of the state it brings to be inconsistent with democratic principles. The neoliberals reject a laissez-faire economy for related though different reasons. They criticize laissez-faire postions, both classical and more recent ones, for overlooking the problems of limitation and control of private economic power.[18] The neoliberals prefer competition because it is a nonauthoritarian means of societal control.[19] Competition policy must have as its object the maintenance of this system. They consider the passive role assigned the state under laissez-faire theories to be inadequate to maintain the competitive system. The neoliberal position, reflected in the German cartel law, calls for "an economy in which the competitive system is maintained by government measures (taxes, currency regulation, credit policy, etc.)."[20] The active maintenance of competition becomes the duty of the state.[21]

The neoliberals thus ascribe a central role to German cartel law in the country's economic law. Since "economic law is the law of controlling the economy,"[22] they recognize the role of competition policy in the direction of the economy. But they oppose making competition policy an instrument of daily economic policy to be altered at will for every particular case. Competition is to provide a limit on private economic power comparable to the limit on state power imposed by the Rule of

Law.[23] All too frequent exemption and exception would destroy that function. A proposed deviation from a competition policy must be studied to determine if the claimed benefits will outweigh the resulting restriction of competition. To the extent competition cannot be realized or is not permitted for political reasons, the neoliberals advocate introduction of a market supervision mechanism to substitute for the control normally provided by competition.[24]

German adoption of a mixed system of administration and adjudication can be seen as the selection of a device to permit implementation of the neoliberal position of "competition as mission."[25] Only through active participation of the state is competition guaranteed; competition is too important an element in control of society to be left to a protective apparatus dependent on private initiation. On the other hand, the stress the neoliberals place on the Rule of Law makes clear that an administrative approach was not adopted to reduce Rule of Law safeguards against the state. Administration is involved where a policy judgment about structuring the economy is demanded. That judgment must be protected from day-to-day political interference, yet it must be ultimately politically responsible, for it is a direction of society.

SCOPE OF THIS WORK

This work proceeds from the observation that German cartel law tries to assign policy judgments to administration, while American antitrust law treats all decisions as matters for judicial justice. It explores how this difference may explain why antitrust decisions in the United States are often thought to force a trade-off between good policy and good law, while in the Federal Republic of Germany there is no comparable perception.

This work investigates the legal methods by which policy decisions are handled under German and American antitrust law. Two questions stand at the center of the investigation: Do the legal methods distort the policy decision? and, Does the policy decision threaten the integrity of antitrust as law?

The plan of the investigation is to begin with consideration of certain fundamental questions: Chapter 2 considers what is meant by policy, what demands the Rule of Law makes on law, and whether policy decisions have special requirements regarding the Rule of Law. Differences between American and German attitudes toward the Rule of

Law are identified insofar as they are relevant to this investigation. Chapter 3 considers whether and when policy decisions are required in German and American antitrust law. It surveys the substantive provisions of the two laws briefly. Chapters 4 to 7 consider the major differences in legal methods and how they interrelate with policy decisions.

As a comparison of law, this work has a limited goal. It seeks to heighten recognition of the interrelation of legal methods and law. It seeks to identify different methodological treatment of policy questions and to suggest the importance of that treatment. It does not seek to describe either law in detail. Accordingly, it does not provide detailed descriptions of methods and of substantive law.

2

The Tension Between the Rule of Law and Policy

In both Germany and the United States, law is believed to have requirements purely its own as law without regard to material content. For law to function satisfactorily as an ordering mechanism in society, it is held to meeting these requirements collectively, even if it cannot always meet each individually. There is hardly agreement on a precise enumeration of these individual requirements, but there is something of an international consensus between the Federal Republic and the United States as to the core essentials. Law should be clear. It should be publicly promulgated and prospective. Law should be stable. A mechanism for its implementation should permit a predictable decision in the individual case. All these requirements help law fulfill an ordering role. They make voluntary compliance with the law possible. Collectively, these requirements are discussed in the United States as the Rule of Law and in the Federal Republic as the legal security (*Rechtssicherheit*) aspect of the *Rechtsstaat* (Rule of Law) principle. In both legal systems these requirements are of critical importance.[26] Lon Fuller called these requirements "the internal morality of law."[27] Gustav Radbruch derived the principle of legal security from the concept of law (*Rechtsidee*).[28]

For this work, two interests of the individual which the Rule of Law safeguards are of central importance: Law must be capable of guiding those subject to it;[29] and, for law to be capable of guiding the subject, it must also protect him from arbitrary use of power to make and apply law. The former is discussed in this work as the guidance interest and the latter as the protection interest. When the Rule of Law is safeguarded, the subject can rely on the law and can foresee application of state power. The securing of the Rule of Law was an important concession sought from the absolutist state by the bourgeoisie, for it makes economic planning possible. Yet the purpose of the Rule of Law is limited. Protection of the Rule of Law only assures the integrity and the regularity of application of the legal rules as such; it does not assure that these rules serve either justice or utility.[30]

In both the Federal Republic of Germany and the United States, the requirements imposed by the Rule of Law are sometimes broken down into two subgroups; in broad outline, these two groups are similar between the two countries. In the Federal Republic, a distinction is made between Rule of Law security in guidance and in realization (*Orientierungs* – and *Realisierungssicherheit*).[31] In the United States, a comparable distinction is made by identification of the relevant legal instrument: rules and the machinery for applying them (sometimes simply courts).[32] In each country, one group of requirements makes demands on the legal rules themselves; the other group makes demands on the institutions charged with implementing the law. Fulfillment of the Rule of Law requires satisfaction of both groups of requirements.

Nevertheless, there seems a different emphasis in the relative importance ascribed these two groups of requirements in the attainment of the Rule of Law. Without saying whether courts or rules are to have the more important role in either country, the relative weighting favors rules more in the Federal Republic of Germany and courts more in the United States.[33]

This different emphasis in the fulfillment of the Rule of Law ideal becomes apparent in this investigation of antitrust law. It is also evident in criminal law and procedure, that is, in an area where the protection interest of the Rule of Law is especially important because of the severity of state intrusion in the life of the subject. In criminal law, German law protects the subject by a precise norm stating offense and punishment under which the accused's act must be painstakingly subsumed.[34] American law, on the other hand, has more haphazard norms – a plethora of overlapping state and federal statutes – but introduces numerous autonomous decision makers, and limits strictly the inculcating evidence they may consider.[35] While this difference in emphasis is noticeable, it is not a difference in kind. In the Federal Republic of Germany and in the United States, both rules and courts are expected to contribute to the fulfillment of the Rule of Law ideals. Occasional shortcomings in one may be compensated for by improvements in the other.

The collective requirements of the Rule of Law cannot be taken as absolutes. All too soon they conflict with the ability to generalize in rules. Radbruch observed this tension: "Legal security requires positive law, but positive law demands application without regard to its justice and utility."[36] Even were knowledge of the present perfect, complete predictability of law such as would fully satisfy the Rule of Law would collide with the problem of law in time. As Oscar Germann emphasized, "The more the law is laid down in precise statutory paragraphs, the faster it goes out of date."[37] Slavish attention only to the requirements of the Rule of Law would be concentration only on the ordering function of law to the exclusion of law's other functions in realization of justice and in promotion of general welfare. The Rule of Law must at times give way to other interests.[38]

But in what way should the Rule of Law give way? And should it give way in the same measure to interests of justice and to interests of the general welfare? The Rule of Law gives way to some extent whenever law is allowed to be less clear, less predictable, or less reliable. Examples are use of general clauses and retrospective legislation. Whether the Rule of Law should give way to interests of justice or of general welfare is a question which often arises in decision of an individual case; then the justice interest is expressed as an appeal to equity and the general welfare interest as an appeal to public policy.

This work uses the concepts of "equity judgments" and "public policy decisions" (or simply "policy") throughout. These concepts describe situations where it is either not possible or not desirable to bind the decision maker in an individual case with strict legal rules. In such cases, where the Rule of Law gives way for the sake of justice in the individual case, an equity judgment arises. Where strict rules are abandoned to permit adjustment of the decision for the sake of general welfare, a public policy decision is indicated.[39] Relying on a concept of Richard Wasserstrom, an equity judgment can be defined as a judgment made, not according to rules, but for the sake of "the best possible result as between the parties at present before the court."[40] Similarly, a public policy decision, in the widest sense, can be defined as a judgment which takes into account and may even prefer interests which are not immediately represented before the court or other decision maker. In this wide sense, a public policy decision necessarily concerns more interests than those immediately represented before the court, but does not necessarily require that the entire society be considered.[41]

In both the Federal Republic of Germany and the United States, interests of public policy are frequently conceded less of a claim to relaxation of Rule of Law guarantees than are interests of equity. In the Federal Republic, for example, Rule of Law security (*Rechtssicherheit*) and justice (*Gerechtigkeit*) are both counted as principal components of the constitutionally guaranteed *Rechtsstaat* principle;[42] utility (*Zweckmäßigkeit*) is not.[43] Radbruch, while deriving Rule of Law security, justice, and utility from the concept of law, placed utility in third position, clearly inferior to the other two.[44] In the United States, Ronald Dworkin would deny public policy a role in the decision of "hard cases," which he understands to be cases where there is no clear binding rule of law.[45]

This relative handicapping of public policy as against equity interests does not deny public policy a role in law. Interests of the general welfare must be considered in law; law cannot be concerned only with justice. Radbruch observed that considerations of justice indicate that the thief should be punished less severely than the murderer, but only considerations of general welfare can suggest what scale of punishments should be applied to both.[46] Public policy is accorded greater importance in creation of law than in its application. Public policy means the current needs of the community. What these needs are is subject to rapid change and to considerable disagreement. When public policy is taken into account only in creation of law, the Rule of Law need not be endangered. The policy decision is made when the legislature lays down what will be law in the future. When policy is not taken into account until decision of an individual case, the Rule of Law is threatened. In such a case the protection interest is compromised in a way in which it is not when the Rule of Law is relaxed for equity reasons. In the former case the holder of state power charged with implementing the law is also authorized to determine what is the general welfare. Rule of Law protection against the state disappears when the state's decision maker can adjust each individual case to his conception of general welfare. In the Nazi dictatorship a simple principle expressed this power: "Everything useful to the people is right; everything that injures them is wrong."[47] In Anglo-American tradition, *the* symbol of violation of the Rule of Law is still the seventeenth century Court of Star Chamber, which, according to Maitland, "was a court of politicians enforcing a policy, not a court of judges administering the law."[48]

A distinction between creation of law and its application becomes problematic when a creative role for judges is recognized in the application of law. German legal theory of the eighteenth and nineteenth centuries denied that judges had such a creative role and thus avoided the problem. In the jurisprudence of interests (*Interessenjurisprudenz*) of the early twentieth century, and even more in the jurisprudence of values (*Wertungsjurisprudenz*) which followed after 1945, judges were expected to consider what purposes of general welfare lay behind a statute, when compelled to choose between different interpretations of it. Judges were not themselves, however, to determine what was the general welfare.[49] In other words, policy questions might enter into the legal interpretation of statutes, but policy judgments should not be made in application of statutes.[50] Policy judgments are matters for administration and not for adjudication.[51]

The Anglo-American legal world today explicitly concedes that judges sometimes create law. If judges are acting like legislators, should they take into account general welfare just like legislators? Dworkin has argued they should not. Dworkin has proposed a theory to deal with "hard cases," which he identifies as those cases where there is no clear, binding rule of law.[52] In his "rights thesis" he argues that judges are bound to decide by principle when there is no binding rule of law. Judges are not to resort to policy in such hard cases, for to do so would be not to take rights seriously. For Dworkin, arguments of principle draw their support from claims of individual or group right; arguments of policy, on the other hand, draw support from claims for furtherance of some collective goal.[53] H.L.A. Hart finds Dworkin's rights thesis a "Nobel Dream." Hart says judges do, and will continue to, take recourse to both arguments of policy and of principle in deciding hard cases. For Hart it is perfectly proper for judges in choosing between two possible answers each supported by existing law, to take into account considerations of general welfare.[54] Hart, it would seem, is not, any more than the modern German schools of jurisprudence, calling for judges themselves to determine what is general welfare and make public policy the rule of decision.[55]

3

Policy in the Implementation of Antitrust Law

A comparison of how the methods of German and American antitrust law handle tensions arising from making policy decisions in their application would, of course, be unnecessary if such policy decisions were never required to apply the law. As discussed in Chapter 2, one way to comport with the requirements of the Rule of Law would be to make all policy decisions before application of the law to the individual case. Indeed, one recurring ideal version of the Rule of Law would eliminate all subjective value judgments, such as policy decisions, from the application of law and permit only objective acts of recognition. This chapter discusses differences between acts of recognition and value judgments and then shows that both German and American antitrust law frequently require policy decisions and other value judgments for their application.

ACTS OF RECOGNITION AND VALUE JUDGMENTS

An act of recognition is an objective determination of a factually described condition. The law which requires an act of recognition mandates that the decision maker apply objective measures. The factual determination required may raise difficult questions of weighing observations, but is merely determinative and is never normative. Such a difficult determination might be, for example, that a break-in occurred "at night." In contrast, a value judgment requires an independent valuing according to a measure not provided by the law.

Policy decisions and equity judgments are both varieties of value judgments. A value judgment requires the decision maker to value an individual situation, that is, for that case, he decides like a legislator. The law does not furnish all the standards necessary for decision, but instead refers to subjective standards which can be applied only once the decision maker adopts a personal standard. For example, the decision maker may be required to decide that a defendant acted recklessly, that a publication is pornographic, or that a zoning variance is in the public interest.

The potential difficulties of such a distinction between acts of recognition and value judgments cannot be expounded here.[56] The distinction is somewhat fluid in that, through descriptive requirements, a value judgment can be converted, at least for a particular decision, into an act of recognition. For example, a zoning law might state that a zoning variance is deemed always to be in the public interest when such a variance permits construction of a licensed pharmacy in a part of town that presently has no licensed pharmacy.

As is shown in the following sections, both German and American antitrust law frequently require the decision maker to judge economic effect on competition. Whether such economic decisions should be viewed as value judgments or as acts of recognition is an important question considered in the last part of this chapter. Until then, economic judgments are spoken of separately from policy judgments, without prejudging their status as value judgments or as acts of recognition.

Policy and Economic Decisions in German Cartel Law

The substantive provisions of German cartel law frequently require the decision maker to reach policy judgments and economic decisions. This point is established by consideration of the major provisions of the GWB; treatment of details, such as of special provisions for certain sectors of the economy, can be omitted. The major substantive provisions of the GWB fall into four principal categories: cartel agreements, other agreements, abusive conduct, and concentration control.[57]

Cartel Agreements

The heart of the GWB is a prohibition of cartel (horizontal) agreements. Contracts concluded for a common purpose and decisions of trade associations are ineffective so far as they "are likely, through restraints on competition, to affect production or market conditions of commerce in goods or commercial services" (§ 1 I 1). Conduct directed to a tacit agreement, which could not legally be effective, is similarly prohibited (§ 25 I). To this seemingly simple prohibition the German legislature has appended a long list of possible exemptions. Before an exemption can apply, some form of review by the cartel authorities is necessary. This review frequently forces the reviewer to reach policy judgments and economic decisions. The most explicit of these general welfare judgments require findings such as: "the arrangement is reached with due regard for the economy generally and for the general welfare" (§ 4 – emergency structural crisis cartels); whether the rationalization is in "the public interest" (§ 5 III 1 – certain rationalization cartels involving agreements on price or on joint procurement or distribution); and "if in an exceptional case the restriction on competition is necessary for more important reasons of the entire economy and the public interest" (§ 8 I – extraordinary exemption general clause). Other exemptions require the reviewer to reach economic decisions about competition generally or about specific aspects of it. Examples of the former include findings such as: "permits substantial competition in the market to continue" (§ 5a I 1 – rationalization by specialization cartels); "if thereby competition in the market is not substantially affected" (§ 5b I – other rationalization cartels for small business); and, "can lead to a substantial restraint on competition domestically and the interest in maintaining competition predominates" (§ 6 III No. 2 – export cartels). Examples of the latter include more specific findings such as: "to increase substantially the efficiency or productivity of the participating enterprises . . . and thereby to improve satisfaction of demand" (§ 5 II 1 – rationalization cartels); "the agreement . . . serves to promote the efficiency of small or middle sized enterprises" (§ 5b I – other rationalization cartels for small businesses); and "the German producers are faced with no or only insubstantial competition on the side of the suppliers" (§ 7 I – import cartels).

Other Agreements

While the GWB needs only one main prohibition (subject to exemptions) to deal with cartel (horizontal) agreements, it requires three different provisions to treat other (mostly vertical) agreements. One rule voids contracts which restrict a participant "in the freedom to establish prices or business terms" in contracting with third parties (§ 15). The

GWB thereby prohibits resale price maintenance; it makes an exception for the book trade (§ 16), but subjects that exception to withdrawal from individual publishers if "resale price maintenance is used abusively" (§ 17 I No. 1). A second rule declares contracts dealing with protected rights, such as patents, ineffective so far as they impose restrictions extending beyond the scope of the right (§ 20 I; certain restrictions are specifically permitted by § 20 II). This rule empowers the cartel authorities to exempt an otherwise ineffective contract in certain circumstances provided that "competition in the market is not substantially affected" (§ 20 III 1). Yet a third rule subjects four other types of contract (exclusive dealing, selective distribution, tie-ins, and limited utilization) to a uniform oversight for abuses (§ 18 I). This rule authorizes cartel authorities to prohibit abuses of these contracts when they are able to make findings such as: "for competition on the market concerned, a considerable number of enterprises are similarly bound" (§ 18 I a); "for other enterprises entry to the market is inequitably restricted" (§ 18 I b); "competition in the market is . . . substantially affected" (§ 18 I c).

Abuse Control

The GWB introduces three different types of controls of abusive economic conduct, which vary according to the addressee: Some apply to all market participants, some only to participants having a position of superiority over certain other participants, and some only to enterprises which dominate the market as a whole. Applicable to all market participants are the prohibitions of boycotts (§ 26 I) and the prohibition of pressure to compel de facto acceptance of contracts forbidden by the GWB (for example, price maintenance) (§ 25 II). Of the second type is a prohibition of inequitable or unjustifiable discrimination; until 1973 it was applicable only to market dominating enterprises, but now applies whenever there is a relation of economic dependency (§ 26 II 2). Also of the second type of control is the power granted the cartel authorities to forbid conduct of enterprises having a superior position as against smaller competitors, provided that the enterprise is in a position to influence market relationships, the competitor is inequitably handicapped, and the conduct "is likely to have a lasting effect on competition" (§ 37a III). The third type of abuse control is the power given the cartel authorities to prohibit abuses of market power by market dominating enterprises. In order to determine that an enterprise is market dominating and to find that it is engaging in abusive conduct, the cartel authorities must reach economic decisions and policy judgments. The GWB defines an enterprise to be market dominating, when it "is without competitors or is exposed to no substantial competition or has a dominating market position in relation to its competitors" (§ 22 I Nos. 1 – 2). Two or more enterprises may share a position of market dominance and thus be subject to the control (§ 22 II). If an enterprise meets certain numerical criteria, it is presumed to be market dominating (§ 22 II). The GWB does not define abuse, but it does give three examples of abuses. Perhaps most interesting is the second, which suggests that the cartel authorities may find an abuse when a market-dominating enterprise imposes business conditions which depart from those "which would with high probability result in the presence of workable competition" (§ 22 IV No. 2). The cartel authorities have invoked the abuse control to prohibit excessive pricing.

Merger Control

Amendments made to the GWB in 1973 inhibit industrial concentration. The amended GWB requires that the Federal Cartel Authority (BKartA – *Bundeskartellamt*) prohibit mergers which it expects to lead to creation or to strengthening of a market-dominating position, unless the participating enterprises prove "also improvements in competitive conditions will occur and that these improvements outweigh the disadvantages of the market domination" (§ 24 I). Should the Federal Cartel Authority prohibit a merger, the GWB requires the federal minister for economics, on application, to grant permission for the merger "if in the particular case the restriction on competition is offset by advantages for the economy generally resulting from the merger or the merger is justified by an overriding public interest" (§ 24 III 1). The GWB requires the minister to take into account the competitive position of the enterprise in markets outside Germany. He may not grant permission for a merger if it would endanger "the free market economy" (§ 24 III 2).

Policy and Economic Decisions in American Antitrust Law

American antitrust law frequently forces the decision maker to reach economic decisions. The role of noneconomic policy judgments, on the other hand, is less clear. Whether and when such general welfare decisions are required has been hotly contested. Only rarely are they explicitly required by statute – notably the new requirement that consent decrees must be in the "public interest."[58] In general, recent case law has tended to deny such noneconomic judgments a place in legal decisions under the antitrust law.[59] Whether such noneconomic judgments have actually been banished from every application of the law is less clear. The Antitrust Division, for example, is probably expected to take such considerations into account in exercise of its prosecutorial discretion;[60] factual findings of other decision makers may be colored by such considerations.

As with German cartel law, a complete exposition of American antitrust law is not necessary. A brief review of its principal provisions is sufficient to show that it frequently compels economic decisions and that it at least presents opportunities for general welfare judgments. Here, three major substantive provisions are considered: the Sherman Act § 1 prohibition of collusion in restraint of trade; the Sherman Act § 2 prohibition of monopolization; and the Clayton Act § 7 control of industrial concentration.[61]

Agreements in Restraint of Trade

Section 1 of the Sherman Act prohibits: "Every contract, combination in the form of trust or otherwise, or conspiracy, in restraint of trade or commerce among the several states, or with foreign nations . . . ." Out of this general clause the federal courts have developed most of American antitrust law. Section 1 is often taken as an authorization for development of a federal common law of trade restraint. Read literally it is thought that it would "outlaw the entire body of private contract law."[62] The language itself is regarded as so broad that "it cannot mean what it says."[63] The federal courts have therefore regarded it as their function to give form and limit to Section 1. The key device in that effort has been the so-called rule of reason, which is often hard for those not trained in the common law to understand.[64]

The rule of reason is a good example for the observation that common law rules often take no single definitive form.[65] Although the rule of reason is traced back to an English decision of 1711[66] and has been part of American antitrust law since at least 1911,[67] it still has no agreed formulation. Only recently Ernest Gellhorn observed that "additional rulings may be necessary before the rule of reason can be accurately summarized."[68] In such instances American lawyers tend to fall back on trying to predict how a majority of the currently sitting Supreme Court justices will view the law. A similar limitation may be made here.

The rule of reason is really no rule at all. Rather than a norm, it is a mandate to conduct an "inquiry."[69] It authorizes the federal courts to judge "whether the challenged agreement is one that promotes competition or one that suppresses competition."[70] The courts rely on what they call "antitrust analysis" to decide whether there is "an unreasonable restraint on competition." This analysis is said inescapably to require consideration of market power.[71] Whether noneconomic grounds may be used to support a judgment that a restraint is reasonable and therefore not violative of Sherman Act § 1 has been contested. That the reasonableness of a restraint may rest on social, but noneconomic benefits, is widely regarded today as an aberrant view, although not without some Supreme Court support in the past.[72] The present Supreme Court takes the position that "the purpose of the analysis is to form a judgment about the competitive significance of the restraint; it is not to decide whether a policy favoring competition is in the public interest, or in the interests of a member of the industry."[73]

To facilitate application of Sherman Act § 1 the federal courts have developed so-called per se rules of antitrust illegality. Today these rules are generally viewed as subcategories of the rule of reason.[74] Where the courts have had "considerable experience"[75] with certain business relationships, the courts may classify them as per se unlawful because "their nature and necessary purpose are so plainly anticompetitive."[76] At one time or another a wide variety of agreements and other concerted activity has been held subject to per se rules. Horizontal agreements on price, market division, and boycotts have been held per se unlawful, as well as vertical arrangements such as resale price maintenance, restrictive distribution by territorial allocation, and certain forms of exclusive dealing.[77]

These per se rules are considerably closer to what a German lawyer thinks of as a norm than is the rule of reason. While generally they are conceded to have greater predictability and ease of application, critics have charged that per se rules threaten a defendant's right to a "full day in court." S. Chesterfield Oppenheim attacked the per se doctrine as possibly "repugnant to these fundamental constitutional safeguards," for it "at once forecloses a [defendant] from introducing evidence on the panoply of possible legal and economic justifications in harmony with an overriding public interest . . . ."[78] Gellhorn observes that ease of judicial application alone cannot justify per se rules: "Fairness and justice normally command that one charged with causing harm have an opportunity to show that such harm has not (or will not) occur."[79] Per se rules are seen as broad generalizations about the social utility of commercial practices; classification as a per se rule requires a judgment of the likely impact on competition for the great majority of such cases. Should later experience prove that earlier judgment erroneous, a particular practice may be reclassified for consideration under the more encompassing rule of reason inquiry.[80] Just as in the application of the rule of reason, then with every creation or abolition of a per se rule there is an economic judgment. On the other hand, in contrast to the rule of reason, economic decisions are not necessary in the application of per se rules.[81]

Monopolization

Section 2 of the Sherman Act prohibits monopolization, attempts to monopolize, and conspiracies to monopolize. Case law has held that monopolization requires proof of possession of monopoly power, while an attempt to monoplize requires proof of a dangerous probability of success.[82] In both instances, the decision maker must reach economic determinations of the extent of defendant's power. He must identify a relevant product and geographic market[83] and must determine the defendant's power in that market.[84] No single economic measure of these factors is legally determinative. If monopolization is found, the decision maker may fashion a remedy which includes dissolution of the corporation concerned. Dissolution requires consideration of the interests of a wide circle of individuals, such as: the corporation's shareholders, its competitors, its customers, its suppliers, and its employees.[85] Where the corporation concerned has a critical role in the national economy, it seems likely that the decision maker will consider that role.

The National Commission for Review of Antitrust Laws and Procedures proposed greater use of the attempted monopolization provision in order to reach conduct which "significantly threatens competition in any relevant market."[86] It suggested doing that by cutting back the dangerous probability of success requirement.

Merger Control

Section 7 of the Clayton Act prohibits mergers "where in any line of commerce in any section of the country, the effect of such acquisition may be substantially to lessen competition, or to tend to create a monopoly." As with the monopolization provision of Sherman Act § 2, Clayton Act § 7 requires the decision maker to construct a relevant product and geographic market.[87] He must then determine the likely effect of the merger on competition in that market. No single economic measure is legally determinative of that effect. In 1968, 1982, and 1984 the Antitrust Division of the Department of Justice issued guidelines spelling out when it would challenge mergers.[88] The federal courts, and indeed the Department of Justice itself, did not treat the 1968 guidelines as determinative of the legal question.[89]

The Supreme Court has refused to consider that a positive effect in one market might outweigh negative effects in another. In so doing, it also rejected a broader, noneconomic consideration of general welfare comparable to the aberrant view of the rule of reason: "A merger is not saved from illegality under § 7 . . . because on some ultimate reckoning of social or economic debits and credits, it may be deemed beneficial."[90]

Economic Decisions and Value Judgments

The many economic decisions required by German cartel law and by American antitrust law should be considered value judgments in the sense in which that term is used in this work. The many judgments of competition that the respective laws require are insufficiently described to be acts of recognition. These decisions require the decision maker to value the individual situation and decide like a legislator; the decision maker cannot merely determine the existence of a factually described condition. Friedrich von Hayek has discussed at length the "essentially subjective character of all economic theory."[91] He has pointed out:

> That the objects of economic activity cannot be defined in objective terms but only with reference to a human purpose goes without saying. Neither a "commodity," or an "economic good", nor "food" or "money", can be defined in physical terms but only in terms of views people hold about things.[92]

Consequently, definitions of markets and judgments about effects on competition cannot, without further description, eliminate the value judgments inherent in the terms. Drawing a product or geographic market can only be a defensible choice.[93] Drawing a market one way is to leave some participants out who belong in; it is a determination that some participants objectively have an adequate substitute, when subjectively they may not.[94] The inherent element of judgment could be eliminated only if the law dictated how to draw the relevant market, a step not yet taken.

Contemporary economic theory explicitly recognizes the subjective element inherent in the term competition. Antitrust law is based on the assumption that competition should control the market. Yet economic theory recognizes that the model of "perfect competition" is rarely, if ever, attainable. Instead, modern economic theory holds that "workable competition" is ordinarily a satisfactory substitute.[95] Of course, not everyone will agree when competition is workable; those not satisfied by the resulting economic allocation are likely to challenge the conclusion that there is workable competition.

Additional problems are presented when the economic judgment is of future effect. Markets are subject to political change independent of economic conditions. Where before an international market assured competition, a foreign war or revolution may bring that control to an end. On the other hand, it may be considered politically or socially necessary to permit a domestic industry to consolidate to achieve economies of scale in the domestic market alone and not force it to rely on an uncertain foreign market. Impending economic or political change may also force a decision as to which market should be kept competitive. Should the competitiveness of a market which serves a clientele or need of declining importance be protected, or should less competition be accepted in that market in order to promote a market having a growing importance?

Antitrust laws might describe the economic decisions they require sufficiently to turn these decisions into acts of recognition, but there is reason to believe that they could not ever do so successfully. Antitrust laws must deal with rapidly changing economic conditions and with the new restraints of trade those changing conditions make possible.[96] Antitrust laws must also deal with the extreme relativity of economic activity. Very few economic acts can be categorically condemned or approved; they must instead be evaluated within the context of the rapidly changing market. Indeed, antitrust laws are often regarded as deliberately adopting vague terms in order to deal with these problems.[97]

When an economic decision is a value judgment, it seems likely, especially if the judgment is about competition generally, that it will be a policy rather than an equity judgment. But it need not always be a policy judgment. In both Germany and the United States competition is said to be protected not only for reasons of economic efficiency, but also for reasons of individual freedom. While the former is a general welfare or policy goal, the latter is normally an equity interest. So far, however, as the decision in a particular case turns on the overall effect on competition and not on the effect on the individual competitor, the standard of decision is general welfare and a policy judgment is indicated. Most decisions about competition in the United States, under the rule of reason or under the Clayton Act, require policy judgments in this sense. The Supreme Court has underscored that "The antitrust laws . . . were enacted for the protection of *competition*, not *competitors*."[98] The goal of antitrust analysis in the United States is the judgment of the threat to "the proper operation of our predominantly free market economy."[99]

4

Legal Limits on Antitrust Policy Decisions

In both the Federal Republic of Germany and the United States, wise antitrust policy is thought to require an antitrust law which permits making value judgments in the course of its implementation. So far as such a law is realized, the concerns expressed by the Rule of Law require asking, What are the legal limits on these judgments? To decide that a policy decision is sometimes required in antitrust proceedings is to recognize implicitly that the law cannot always provide the exact answer. Yet if the law is to provide guidance to the citizen and protection from the arbitrary use of power,[100] the law must limit that antitrust policy decision. The natural question is: How is the antitrust policy decision circumscribed?

Karl Engisch observes that binding to statute is a matter of degree – of more or less.[101] The law cannot invariably provide the correct answer. Here, it is useful to observe a relativity of binding in yet another way. Binding is both positive and negative. It is probably more usual to think of binding in a positive sense: What decision does the law require in this case? But binding exists in a negative sense as well: What decision does the law preclude in this case? Both the guidance and the protection functions of the Rule of Law can be satisfied by negative binding, even when positive binding is only very weak or nonexistent. To be sure, positive binding, which establishes exactly what the legal decision must be, provides the highest measure of legal certainty. But negative binding can inform the citizen who wants guidance in planning and knowledge of the legal risks, what steps he can take toward safety, and where he will be secure from government challenge. This phenomenon is readily apparent in areas of economic planning, where it is not uncommon to observe that what the law is is less important than that it is certain, for so long as the law is clear, one can plan accordingly.[102]

German and American antitrust law vary less in the measure of positive binding each manages than they differ in the degree of negative binding each delivers. As shown in Chapter 3, both laws often deliberately do not bind decision makers positively. But when German cartel law does not bind decision makers positively, it does bind them negatively. American antitrust law, on the other hand, negatively binds decision makers only weakly, if at all. Those limits which elsewhere bind common law decisions negatively function imperfectly or not at all in antitrust law.

BINDING IN THE UNITED STATES: PRECEDENT AND STARE DECISIS

A lawyer in a common law country such as the United States, if asked what is the legal limit on judicial decision, is apt to respond instinctively – precedent. A precedent is a previously decided case. In the precedent the lawyer discovers the ratio decidendi (or ratio, for short). This ratio, according to the doctrine of stare decisis, is binding in subsequent cases. The ratio thus seems to have the central role in determining the binding force of precedent; indeed, in England a substantial literature is addressed to this point. Julius Stone has said that in a system of law founded on stare decisis, the task of identifying and delimiting this decisum is "the deepest secret of juristic life."[103] The ratio is the reason for deciding. It is the constellation of material facts and law which together justify the decision of the issue in the particular case; it is all that a court must have decided in order to decide the instant case and nothing the court need not have decided.[104] Stone has suggested that two senses of the term ratio decidendi should be distinguished: The descriptive ratio, which describes the process of reasoning by which the decision is reached, and the prescriptive ratio, which identifies and delimits the reasoning which a later court is bound to follow. Only the prescriptive ratio binds judicial decision. Depending upon the method by which the ratio is determined, the descriptive ratio[105] can be broader or narrower than the prescriptive ratio.

Here it is not necessary to delve into the mysteries of how the lawyer discovers the ratio decidendi; it is sufficient to discuss a few of its important characteristics and point out its particular role in American law. In common law systems the ratio is generally deliberately limited; the court is deciding just this one case, perhaps just this one issue. Karl Llewelyn likened the rule provided by the ratio to a starting point in an otherwise empty field. He suggested that the norm of German law can be seen as a line drawn around a certain region, while the ratio is but one point.[106] From this point, lawyers may in later cases proceed to resolve other controversies. If the later case matches the first, then the ratio provides the solution. The precedent can be said to be binding. If not, then the lawyer must, as Edward Levy has observed, consider whether there is a rule, of which this earlier precedent is an example, and which will encompass the later dispute as well. In other words, the lawyer moves analogically to extend the earlier ratio to cover the facts of the new controversy.[107]

The rules which develop from this procedure tend to be narrowly bound factually. They are more certain where there are more repeated instances of similar controversies. Llewelyn observed that, even where such a rule is considered clear and long standing, it rarely takes on one precise verbal form.[108] The system thus remains open to incorporate problems which arise in future controversies. As the points covered by the ratios become more numerous, the rule becomes clearer, but it still does not set strict limits. Areas not covered are left free to deal with future controversies as necessary to decide those cases. The precedent provides first a rule of decision, and only incidentally a norm. In Llewelyn's words, the common law rule is a guideline (*Richtlinie*) and not a premise (*Vordersatz*).[109]

No Strict Binding to Precedent

Precedent serves less to inform the public about its rights and duties than to help lawyers decide future controversies. While the German lawyer tends to think of law as norms, the traditional common law lawyer is just as likely to think first of the concrete controversy between two parties before he looks for a rule. A court follows its precedents, because if it does, it helps the lawyers appearing before it predict the decision of the controversy. It helps the lawyers settle the case themselves without the court; it helps them reduce the points at issue between them, and thereby avoid litigation costs and risks and thus spare the court time. The precedent of the superior court similarly guides the inferior court in its decision. Because precedent serves primarily to guide the decision maker (rather than the party subject to the decision), precedent rules are to be followed unless some reason exists not to – for example, this controversy presents some different element that distinguishes it from the previous controversy.[110] In such cases, the original decision maker would presumably adopt a different rule. Generally, the more frequently a rule has been followed, or the more likely it is that a party has relied upon it, the more reason there is for the court to continue to adhere to it.

At times in the history of the common law, precedent has been said to bind the judicial decision strictly. In England, toward the end of the eighteenth century, the idea became dominant that a court could not decide against even its own precedent.[111] Arthur Goodhart examined all the arguments for the binding force of individual precedent and found the only persuasive explanation to be legal certainty.[112] In the United States, a strict theory of binding precedent comparable to that in England has never prevailed; a court could always overrule its own precedents.[113] Today, the idea that a court could not overrule its own precedents could only be subject to ridicule.[114] Perhaps this history explains why the discussion of the ratio in the United States has never achieved the same dimension as in England, where the courts have considered themselves strictly bound by precedent.[115] In American law, stare decisis is more a working practice than a hard and fast rule. Legal argument, therefore, soon turns from debating what is the ratio of an opinion and distinguishing what is not (the so-called dicta), to the real question: Is this case a reasonable one in which to reconstrue or modify the rule.

While in the appellate court a precedent provides a rule of decision that is followed for the sake of consistency, in the lower court precedent of an immediately superior court does have binding force. But even here, the role of precedent is primarily guidance for and not restriction of decision makers. In the United States today, a lower court is expected not to let itself be "bound" unwisely. It should deviate from obsolete precedents, if it reasonably believes that the superior court would depart from the old precedent.[116] Similarly, a federal court, when it decides an issue of state law (in a so-called diversity case) decides "correctly," when it decides as the supreme court of the relevant state would decide today, even if that means departing from precedent.[117] For all these purposes, the distinction between what is ratio and what is not does not have the same importance in American as it does in English law. Stone's prescriptive ratio is not as important in the United States because the ratio has less a binding function; more important is the descriptive ratio, for it helps the lower court and the lawyers decide how the higher court would decide today.

"Interstitial Limits"

That precedent does not lead to strict bonds on the judicial decision is not generally considered a drawback in the United States today. Rather, it is seen as a strength of common law methods. The absence of strong bonds permits the court to do justice in the individual case unencumbered by rules that may not have anticipated the peculiarities of the particular case; it allows the law to meet changing needs without being unduly retarded by rigid rules that have little relevance to the new situation. The lack of a strict bond is not thought to turn the judicial decision over to the free whim of the judge. Besides professional constraints on the judge himself, precedents are thought to limit the judicial decision. The judge is freed, it is true, to reach his own value judgment, but only within the interstices of an existing system.[118]

What are these interstitial limits that constrain the common law judge? In the first place, certain factual situations are fairly simple and repetitive. Firm solutions have been reached for them and the judge could not easily decide otherwise. Here the judge is positively bound where the case at hand matches the old precedent. There are relatively many of these points. Indeed, there are so many that, even where the case at hand does not match one, the judge cannot go far before he bumps up against one of them. These points limit the judicial decision if not positively, at least negatively. Both Oliver Wendell Holmes and Rupert Cross noted, for example, that a common law judge could hardly decide against the doctrine of consideration no matter how appealing a particular case might make such a decision.[119]

Between these points, the judge is not entirely free in his decision either. He must cast his decision in general terms. Unless he is prepared to formulate a completely new rule, he will try to state his rule of decision so that it incorporates both the case at hand and an already existing point. In the most common situation, the judge is deciding a controversy about competing claims of right. Rights and duties are correlates. If the judge extends one, he must extend the other. This means that before he can extend one rule too far, he will bump into another, which he may have to restrict if he is to decide as he wishes. Public opinion, and for a lower court, appellate review, make it difficult to cut far into an acknowledged right.[120]

Within these interstices, the judge is expected to behave predictably. For Benjamin Cardozo, judges could be allowed interstitial legislation, not only because the gaps are small, but also because the judge can fall back on considerations of justice in filling in those gaps. Cardozo thought that hardship is not worked on the parties affected by such "interstitial legislation," because "the feeling is that nine times out of ten, if not oftener, the conduct of right-minded men would not have been different if the rule embodied in the decision had not been announced by statute in advance."[121] Nor are these ideas of justice merely the personal philosophies of individual judges. In the American common law system, even where precedent provides no "binding" rule, precedents always provide guidance in the form of principles. Principles give expression to ideas of justice in the law, although they do not take the form of rules and do not make claim to bind the decision of an individual case.[122]

BINDING IN AMERICAN ANTITRUST LAW

The Binding of Precedent

Precedent provides little positive binding of American antitrust policy decisions. Crucial policy questions in many antitrust cases are definition of relevant market and determination of effect on competition. Depending upon how these questions are classified, the doctrine of precedent and stare decisis either does not apply or does so most imperfectly. Furthermore, although antitrust law decisions determine national policy, only Supreme Court decisions, of which there are very few, are binding nationally.

Antitrust Policy Decisions as Questions of Law or of Fact

Precedent and stare decisis is a doctrine of law and therefore does not apply directly to factual questions. Answers to factual questions depend solely on the observations of the fact finder in the first instance.[123] Its decisions are subject only to an indirect control by precedent: An appellate court may decide, that as a matter of law, no reasonable fact finder could have answered the question the way this fact finder did, on the basis of the testimony it heard.[124] This control goes more to what evidence the fact finder heard and less to how the fact finder valued it.[125]

For purposes of the doctrine of precedent and stare decisis, any given antitrust policy decision might be classified as a question of fact or a question of law, or as a question of mixed fact and law.[126] If the decision policy is classified as a pure factual question, then it is not subject to the doctrine of precedent and stare decisis, other than in the indirect fashion just mentioned. When this is the case, precedent is unlikely to limit the policy decision significantly. Precedent limits factual questions only where the record is clear and straightforward and there is so little evidence supporting the finding, that a distant reviewer can confidently reverse the decision of the judge or jury who actually heard the evidence. Although ordinary factual questions have straightforward answers and may permit distant evaluation of evidence, economic questions, such as effect on competition, defy simple characterization. The conclusions of the fact finder should almost always be at least representable, and thus, should be able to escape the no reasonable fact finder test. Definition of the relevant market is said to be such a question of fact.[127]

If an antitrust policy decision is classified as a question of law or as a mixed question of law and fact, it will be subject to the doctrine of precedent and stare decisis. Yet, in view of the complexity involved in economic judgments such as of relevant markets and effects on competition, merely to designate a prior decision as binding can do little to restrict subsequent decisions. Repetition of exactly the same markets and competitive effects is rare; opportunities for distinguishing one case from another are numerous. As a result, in the terminology of Stone used earlier, possibilities for divergence of the prescriptive from the descriptive ratio are practically infinite. Meaningful positive binding therefore must in all probability require further breaking down of the binding elements involved in drawing a market or in measuring effects on competition. This may require making the economic methods used in answering these questions into positive law.

Binding Effect of Economic Methods of Measurement

The extent to which economic methods of market definition and competition measurement should be treated as positive law is a difficult question in American antitrust law. To maximize predictability of the judicial judgment, the methods used to draw the market and measure competition should be foreordained. Maximum predictability requires that one method be recognized as determinative. Yet designation of one method of measurement as determinative is a gross simplification of economic theory. Moreover, to prescribe even one method in adequate detail to determine the result in one case may make that method wholly inapposite in another case. Finally, to make one method determinative is to foreclose later use of further refinements made possible by developments in economic theory.

An example of this dilemma is the treatment of vertical mergers. In *Brown Shoe* v.*United States,*[128] the Supreme Court identified a range of possible factors for determination of the effect on competition. In subsequent cases, courts have selected from this range of factors, tending to give one factor predominant effect, but have not felt completely bound by any one. Although they have been reluctant to rely on factors not identified in the *Brown Shoe* decision, they have not entirely foreclosed use of other factors.[129]

Predictability necessarily suffers the more options are available for determination of these economic questions. One recent decision illustrates the extraordinary difficulties American courts have encountered in trying to deal with this question. In *United States* v. *American Cyanamid Co.* the trial court, the United States District Court for the Southern District of New York, following the urging of the Antitrust Division of the Department of Justice, did not utilize the "standard framework of analysis" of the *Brown Shoe* decision to determine the effect of a vertical merger on competition, but instead relied on "contemporary economic theory." The Court of Appeals for the Second Circuit reversed, holding that "it was error to apply 'contemporary economic theory' to the extent it may be distinct from precedent, and to fail to apply the standard framework of analysis."[130] Although denying the trial court the opportunity to resort to other measures, in the same decision the Court of Appeals nevertheless acknowledged that it had itself added other factors to be considered in measuring effect on competition alongside those already mandated in *Brown Shoe.*

The Limited Number of Nationally Binding Precedents

In American legal theory precedents have claim only to bind inferior courts. In the federal judicial system, which applies the antitrust laws, all inferior courts are bound to decisions of the Supreme Court, but the inferior courts are bound only to the decisions of the intermediate courts in their circuits. Other aspects of this question, which is basically one of organization, are treated in Chapter 7, but the question is mentioned now as it impacts on precedent. Inasmuch as the Supreme Court decides fewer than 200 cases with opinion each year in all fields of law combined, and ordinarily fewer than five in antitrust, the intermediate appellate courts, the thirteen Courts of Appeals, usually have the last word. Their precedents are the binding directions to the lower courts actually trying the cases. Decisions in other circuits are "persuasive," but not binding authority.[131] It often happens, however, that decisions of these different courts may differ widely one from another. The problems this creates in planning for enterprises operating in several circuits are obvious: what appears to be legal in one circuit may appear to be illegal in another.

The Negative Binding of Interstitial Limits

American courts have developed few interstitial limits that effectively restrict antitrust policy decisions and fulfill the guidance and protection interests of the Rule of Law. As already shown, interstitial limits are a product of a large network of firm points. From one of these firm points the judge reaches out to develop a rule for decision. He cannot go too far, however, because he soon runs into other points. As he goes out from that firm point, he is guided by ideas of justice.

There is no large field of firm points in antitrust law. Firm points lead to firm, albeit, narrow rules. Repetitiveness and constancy promote this development. Yet in antitrust law, factual situations are often quite complicated, and therefore repetition is difficult. Because policy decisions are often required, constancy is only sometimes attained. What is in the general welfare must be subject to reassessment with changing social needs. In antitrust law, to the extent there is repetitiveness and constancy, it is in the so-called per se rules.[132] But in the recent case of *Continental T.V. Inc.* v. *GTE Sylvania Inc.*,[133] the Supreme Court made clear, in overruling the only ten-year-old per se rule of *United States* v. *Arnold, Schwinn & Co.*,[134] that per se rules are "broad generalizations" about "social utility" themselves subject to correction as necessary.[135]

That the points of antitrust law themselves are not especially firm does not necessarily foreclose the possibility that antitrust policy decisions are in other ways subject to interstitial limits. General contract and corporation law could impose interstitial limits on antitrust policy decisions, and, to an extent, probably do. Yet, they have not furnished limits which give the security found in other areas where common law methods have achieved more acceptance. In part this is because of the nature of antitrust law and of general contracts and corporate law in the United States. While the former is predominantly federal, the latter is largely still state law. Under American constitutional law, federal law preempts state law. Thus, federal antitrust policy decisions easily override state law.[136] Indeed, where courts have tried to uphold state law against federal antitrust law claims, they have contributed further uncertainty to the scope of antitrust law.[137]

Not only does antitrust law in the United States have a claim sufficient to override state law, it also has claims to override other potential interstitial limits arising from federal law. In the ordinary resolution of a private dispute, the right/duty correlative relation makes it difficult to extend one too far without limit. In antitrust, even though a case may be cast as a private dispute resolution, the rule of decision resolves a question of policy. The duty on which the plaintiff bases his case is not a duty to him, but a duty to general welfare. A claim of general welfare easily expands itself to trump competing claims.[138] Indeed, in order to prevent all arms of government from overreaching in the name of general welfare, many countries have adopted bills of rights.[139]

The fewer firm points antitrust law delivers, the more likely it is that analogical development from any one of those points will be unsatisfactory. If there are only a few potential points from which to work, judges may have to work from points that have only superficial similarities to the case in question.[140] Yet superficial similarities may lead only to unsatisfactory policy decisions. For example, although both are monopolies, the effect on general welfare of a monopoly of pecans is quite different from that of a monopoly of steel.

Within the gaps, Cardozo calls for judges to look to considerations of justice to move from firm points to cover new ground.[141] Yet, in American antitrust law, judges are to decide policy, not justice. Can a principle of policy provide the same degree of guidance to judges and to the public that a principle of justice does?[142] Perhaps it could, if everyone agreed on the applicable principle of policy and how it should be applied. This may be the hope of advocates of a single goal policy for antitrust law.[143] Yet, there should be no surprise if there is less general agreement and far more dispute as to just what is general welfare. More argument about general welfare than about individual equity can be expected, not only because there is apt to be more argument about correct policy than correct justice, but also because welfare decisions usually affect more people than do equity decisions, which resolve only a single conflict between a few parties. Furthermore, equity decisions often affect only the past, while policy judgments usually determine future policy.

Development of interstitial limits, which provide security in other areas of common law, is therefore retarded in antitrust law. Precedent as a system of limitation seems to require many firm points from which one can proceed to decide future cases. It does not appear that antitrust law can ever provide such certain points.

These difficulties with antitrust law lead to asking whether policy decisions should ever be subject to the doctrine of precedent and stare decisis. To follow a precedent means to stand by the past. It is not ordinarily desirable to stay true to a past decision any longer than that past decision continues to have validity for the present and for the future. In this regard, it may be desirable to recognize a difference between policy decisions and equity judgments. While ideas of equity are subject to change, they may alter less rapidly than ideas of general welfare. It may be undesirable to concede policy decisions generally the same durability as equity judgments, unless they are explicitly given validity as political judgments.

OTHER LIMITS IN AMERICAN LAW GENERALLY AND THEIR ABSENCE IN ANTITRUST LAW

Precedent is not the only limit on judicial decision in common law countries. Historically, when traditional common law methods developed, these other limits were quite important. Here, three other limits are considered. Their absence in American antitrust law may suggest a reason why popular dissatisfaction with antitrust law is greater than with other areas of American law. Not unrelated are the indirect limits which arise through the manner of application of the law (considered in Chapter 6) or through control of the decision maker himself (considered in Chapter 7).

Restricted Decisional Authority

The common law court is limited by its grant of authority.[144] On the legal side, limited authority restricts the court to reasoning from only a limited number of legal starting points. On the factual side, limited authority lets the court resolve only controversies.[145] In the nineteenth century, when traditional common law methods predominated, judges' authority was limited by forms of action. A party could have a controversy resolved only if he could bring it under or have it analogized to one of a limited number of possible recoveries. The recoveries were ordinarily possible only where there was an obvious material damage or where there was a disputed claim of right. Limited starting points meant that a claim that could not arguably be asserted under the form of action chosen by the party could be dismissed without trial upon motion of the opposing party.[146]

Antitrust law does not circumscribe the authority given the judge. It does not restrict the judge either to a small number of narrowly defined legal starting points, or to a clearly defined factual controversy. The general clause statement of the Sherman Act and the broad terms of the Clayton Act are virtual invitations to bring before the judge all manner of potential claims, to have him consider the effect of a particular practice on competition.[147] The judge, who is subject to a duty of decision, must decide whether the defendant unreasonably restrained competition. The Sherman Act itself excludes no one and no act from the possibility of unreasonably restraining competition. It requires no particular relation between plaintiff and potential defendant, though the Supreme Court[148] has recently taken some steps toward limiting the circle of potential parties that can claim damage. In general though, perhaps thanks to the nature of the antitrust claim as a duty to general welfare, it is very easy for a plaintiff to get into court. If plaintiff has apparently experienced some economic damage, and if defendant has engaged in some economic practice potentially labelled a restraint, then the courts are inclined to give to plaintiff the chance to show that defendant unreasonably restrained trade.

Limited Number of Available Remedies

Common law judges were limited not only in their authority to consider various factual situations, they were also limited in the remedies they could order. Until the merger of the courts of law and of the courts of equity in the nineteenth century, common law judges had only the power of the sheriff at their disposal. The remedies they could order were only three: a money judgment (which could be enforced by property seizure), a transfer of property (effected by seizure), or an ejectment. This was a real limit on the common law judicial judgment and a reason for the growth of the court of equity.[149]

In view of the combination of law and equity courts, there are now few limits on the remedial scope of antitrust policy decisions. The Sherman Act itself permits sanctioning every violation with three years' imprisonment, treble damages, and an equity decree.[150] The equity decree has a potentially vast scope, since it is based upon a duty, not to a particular plaintiff, but to general welfare. The decree is supposed to be sufficient to remedy the violation. But how far may it go to restore competition? The presidentially created National Commission for Review of Antitrust Laws and Procedures recommended: "Whenever a violation of the antitrust law involving market power has been shown, courts should order relief that will effectively limit that power."[151] In American civil procedure, the court may grant an equity decree when the remedy at law is inadequate. Normally, that is the case when monetary damages will not adequately remedy the injury. In antitrust law, because the injury is to general welfare, the remedy at law is likely to be inadequate, and thus the courts are free to do what is necessary to restore competition.

Statute

In America, statutes perform a significant role in limitation of judicial decision. Statutes intrude on the work of judges to such an extent that there are now only a few narrow areas where judges alone are completely responsible for the law.[152] Although statutes are drafted and applied in a much different way in the United States than they are in Germany, still they significantly limit judicial decision.

While the American antitrust laws ostensively take the form of statutes, in fact antitrust law is widely thought one of the purest examples of judge-made law in the United States. The antitrust statutes are considered grants of authority to the federal courts to develop a common law of trade restraint.[153] The antitrust statutes themselves, true to a role as grants of authority, place only a few limits on antitrust policy decisions; today they do little to limit policy decisions.

All of the antitrust statutes do require proof of an effect on commerce among the several states. This requirement was once a significant limit, because the federal power to regulate commerce permitted by the Constitution was considered limited.[154] As the acknowledged scope of that power has extended, the statutory requirement has become meaningless. The requirement persists, but only works to clutter antitrust trials.[155] Sherman Act § 1 requires a contract, combination, or conspiracy; it therefore requires the involvement of two parties for a violation. The connection between those two parties need not be very firm; indeed, Sherman Act conspiracy has long been in the forefront of widening the definition of conspiracy generally.[156] Finally, Sherman Act § 2 requires a monopoly, or an attempt to achieve a monopoly. Some critics think that free application of the latter requirement has reduced the utility of the former as a limit on the judicial decision.[157]

BINDING TO STATUTE IN GERMAN LAW GENERALLY

A lawyer in Germany is apt to think first of statute as the legal limit on judicial or administrative decision. Binding the state authority to statute is a central element in the German ideal of the *Rechtsstaat*. It is explicitly adopted in Article 20 of the German constitution: "the executive and the administration of justice are bound to statute and justice" (*Gesetz und Recht*). Its practical implementation is a central task of modern German theory of legal method.

The *Rechtsstaat* ideal is usually traced to reaction to the so-called *Kabinettsjustiz* of the absolutist monarchs of the eighteenth century. The Enlightenment brought demands for a fully clear and predictable legal system, which would eliminate all arbitrariness (or cabinet interference) from the application of law. Strict binding of the judge to the statute became the goal, while elimination of all judicial creativity became a sought-after by-product. The Prussian general code of 1794 (*Allgemeines Landrecht* – ALR) used over 19,000 paragraphs to try to answer every conceivable contingency. Its judges were to apply the law to the facts mechanically (*automatenhaft*) – to subsume the individual case under the appropriate statutory provision – and to serve as the "mouthpiece" (*Sprachrohr*) or as the "slave" (*Sklave*) of the statute.[158] The ALR forbad its judges to interpret it and directed them to refer questions of interpretation to a special legislative commission, §§ 47, 49 ALR.

The ALR failed in its attempt to deny all judicial creativity: Prussian judges were soon released to interpret the law. The modern history of German theory of legal methods begins here[159] and often seems a struggle between effectuating a binding of the judge to statute and avoiding the negative effects of an excessive binding. Engisch notes that already in the nineteenth century the concept of strict binding of the judge to statute was shaken and given up as *the* ideal.[160] In this century, the arguments of the free law school (*Freirechtsschule*) were probably less influential in forcing further rethinking of binding of judges to statute than was the shock of the Nazi dictatorship, which posed the problem of "statutory injustice" (*gesetzliches Unrecht*).[161]Binding to statute alone "statute is statute" (*Gesetz ist Gesetz*) demanded correction. Legal certainty could not be an absolute value which could override all interests of justice. Accordingly, Article 20 of the constitution binds the government not to statute (*Gesetz*) alone, but to "statute and justice" (*Gesetz und Recht*). The German Federal Constitutional Court has given Radbruch's cautious resolution of the problem recognition: "positive law, secured by statute and state authority, has priority, even if in content it is unjust and impractical (*unzweckmäßig*), unless the contradiction between the positive statute and justice reaches such an intolerable degree, that the statute must give way to justice as 'false law' (*unrichtiges Recht*)."[162] In the Federal Republic of Germany today no serious jurist questions that application of statutes requires value judgments. Binding the decision maker to statute must be a matter of degree. On the other hand, that Article 20 binds the decision maker to statute and justice (*Gesetz und Recht*) does not release him from binding to statute. A leading textbook explains that binding to statute requires that judges not decide contrary to statute. Judges are bound, not to the mere words of the statute, but to its "sense and purpose" (*Sinn und Zweck*). Finding this limit is the task of statutory interpretation.[163]

The Norm as *Tatbestand* and Legal Consequence

According to prevailing German method, the judge applies a legal norm (the *Rechtssatz*) to a factual situation (the *Sachverhalt*); that is, he subsumes the factual situation under an appropriate legal norm in syllogistic fashion. This is by no means thought to be a mechanical process. The actual subsumption is thought the easiest part of the task. The art of the judge lies in bringing the objective law and the factual world together in preparation for the eventual subsumption. The judge must clarify the factual situation. He must identify and fashion the correct legal norm; only rarely can he read it directly out of the statute. In the judge's application of the law, the legal norm is the major premise, the factual situation the minor premise, and the judge's judgment the conclusion.

Karl Larenz has explained subsumption. A complete legal norm consists of two parts, a *Tatbestand* and a legal consequence (*Rechtsfolge*). The *Tatbestand* (plural *Tatbestände*) is a general description of a particular situation. The legal norm thus takes the form: whenever *Tatbestand* (T) is realized in a concrete factual situation, then a certain legal consequence (R) (*Rechtsfolge*) applies. This is the major premise. The minor premise is that this particular factual situation S fulfills the requirements of the *Tatbestand* T, that is, it is a case of T. The conclusion then logically follows that for the factual situation S, legal consequence R applies. Larenz has represented this, the simplest case of subsumption, symbolically as follows:

$$\begin{array}{ll} T \rightarrow R & \text{(For T – that is, for every case T – R applies)} \\ \underline{S \ = \ T} & \text{(S is a case of T)} \\ S \rightarrow R & \text{(For S, R applies).} \end{array}$$ [164]

Here the possible variations of subsumption which can be built from this basic model (as, for example, where the law provides for exceptions) need not be considered, but how the judge fashions the legal norm must be discussed.

As already seen, the norm consists of a *Tatbestand* and a legal consequence. The *Tatbestand* is made up of any number of appropriate elements (*Tatbestandsmerkmale*). To assemble the norm, the judge usually has to resort to so-called helping norms. These supply or help define elements of the legal norm which the judge may apply. To fashion a norm capable of subsumption, the judge must resort to interpretation of the statute, where it is unclear, and engage in "finding law" (*Rechtsfindung*), where the statute has gaps. The filling out of so-called "indefinite legal concepts" (*unbestimmte Rechtsbegriffe*) has created particular difficulties for subsumption.

Indefinite Legal Concepts; Discretion

The problems of the binding force of indefinite legal concepts (*unbestimmte Rechtsbegriffe* also sometimes called "indefinite statutory concepts" *unbestimmte Gesetzesbegriffe*) and the question of discretion are often discussed together in German literature. The two raise similar problems in that in both cases the statute does not deliver a single definitive answer.

German statutes frequently use indefinite legal concepts in order to take into account the many sides of life that do not lend themselves to definition in clearly defined concepts. The German Constitutional Court has repeatedly held that the use of indefinite legal concepts does not by itself violate the Rule of Law guarantees of binding to statute and justice.[165]

Indefinite legal concepts are usually classified in two categories: descriptive and normative. Descriptive concepts relate to objects and events in the physical world, such as darkness; they are empirical. Normative concepts lack this relation to reality, but require value judgments, such as, what constitutes "good faith" (*Treu und Glauben*) or "good morals" (*gute Sitten*). Some scholars suggest that descriptive concepts create problems only in application but not in interpretation, while normative concepts create problems already in interpretation; according to this view, interpretation and application cannot be separated in the usual way for normative concepts.[166]

Indefinite legal concepts reduce predictability of decision and therefore certainty for the citizen. Some scholars have vigorously argued that indefinite legal concepts give the official charged with applying them a certain room for judgment (*Beurteilungsspielraum*). These scholars contend that indefinite legal concepts require the decision maker to come to the answer he considers the correct one, but, because of lacking definiteness, different decision makers applying the same indefinite legal concepts to the same factual situation can reach different conclusions. These scholars urge, particularly in reference to review of administrative action by an administrative court, that the reviewing court should not substitute its judgment, when the judgment of the administration is a representable decision. According to this view, the interpretation of the indefinite legal concept is subject to review, but not its application.[167] This view of a relative binding force for indefinite legal concepts is controversial. Many administrative and appellate courts have held that indefinite legal concepts bind the decision maker to one correct solution just as any other legal concept even if the difficulty of identifying that solution may give the decision maker a certain room for judgment de facto.[168]

Sometimes the statute deliberately does not bind the decision maker to one correct decision, but leaves him room to reach his own decision based on his own responsibility and independent choice. This is discretion. It is used to permit a purposeful and just decision in the individual case.[169] What is probably the prevailing view in Germany today holds that discretion is appropriate only on the legal consequence, but not on the *Tatbestand* side of the legal norm. That is, discretion in choice of action is appropriate, but not in determination of the prerequisites for action. Otto Bachof uses this distinction to mark the difference between indefinite legal concepts and discretion: the former leaves room for judgment in the prerequisites of action, while the latter provides for freedom of action.[170]

Discretion is of several types. When the decision maker is required to act under so-called *muß* (must) provisions, he is strictly bound and has no discretion. The weakest form of discretion is granted by so-called *soll* (should) provisions. Here the statute requires a particular legal consequence for all typical instances of a given *Tatbestand*, but allows the decision maker to make occasional exceptions in atypical cases. The widest grant of discretion is the so-called "free" discretion, usually granted by provisions using words such as *darf* (may) or *kann* (can).[171] Under German law, exercise of discretion is never really "free" in the sense that it may be exercised at the whim of the decision maker. Rather all discretion is *pflichtgemäß* [172] that is, it must be exercised in accord with the sense and purpose of the statute. Section 40 of the German Administrative Procedure Law (*Verwaltungsverfahrensgesetz* – VwVfG) explicitly provides that when an administrative authority is authorized to act according to its discretion, "it must exercise its discretion in accordance with the purpose of the authorization and must observe the statutory limits of the discretion."

In order to assure the proper exercise of discretion, administrative courts review administrative action. Section 40 of the German Law Governing Administrative Courts (*Verwaltungsgerichtsordnung* – VwGO) guarantees access to these courts in all cases of controversy of public law, excepting constitutional questions (which are directed to the constitutional court) and other controversies where another statute expressly refers the controversy to another court. The controversy must relate to a question of legal relations between the parties. Unless the statute specifically provides otherwise, ordinarily a party can raise a claim only if he is injured in his legal rights, VwGO § 42 II. An affected party can challenge not only positive action founded on discretion, but also inaction.[173]

An exercise of discretion can be challenged in the administrative courts on only two grounds: that the action is outside the limits set by the statute, or, that the action constitutes an abuse of discretion. The utility of the action cannot be challenged before the administrative courts. Thus the administrative courts may not strike down administrative action merely because they think a better solution possible. Rather they must find either an overstepping of discretion (*Ermessensüberschreitung*) or an abuse of discretion (*Ermessensmißbrauch*). The former occurs when the administrative authority, whether by action or by inaction, exceeds the limits of its discretion. In certain cases the discretion of the authorities can be so limited that only one possible result is proper; in such cases then, even though there is theoretically discretion, the administration is in fact positively bound. In other cases, statute sets only a negative bound. An abuse of discretion occurs when the authority's exercise of discretion does not accord with the purposes of the grant of discretion. For example, an exercise of discretion is abusive when it is exercised for personal reasons (for example, for a friend) or for other reasons not relevant to the grant (for example, a police order for fiscal reasons).

Different Justifications for Unbinding the Decision Maker

Binding to statute in German law thus ranges from positive binding, requiring a particular decision, through to negative binding, setting limits on the exercise of discretion. Deficiencies in abilities to foresee future events dictate relaxing strict binding and permitting value judgments in application of law. In German law a relaxing of binding to statute is considered appropriate, above all, in order to permit administrative authorities to make policy-oriented decisions upon their own responsibility; they may choose on the basis of current and local interests among several possibilities. This freedom is acceptable because administrative authorities are politically responsible. Where statute does not bind administrative authorities, they are nonetheless obligated to exercise that freedom in the public interest. Relaxation of binding to statute for judicial decision, on the other hand, is preferably limited to situations where necessary to permit judges to do justice in individual cases. Judges are not politically responsible; they are guaranteed independence to permit them to do justice.[174]

BINDING IN GERMAN CARTEL LAW

Anyone who comes to German cartel law hoping to find a thoroughly consistent codex in which judges simply look up answers to antitrust questions and then apply them mechanically, without interpretation, in the fashion hoped for by the drafters of the Prussian ALR, will be sorely disappointed. The German GWB does not codify prohibited and permitted practices. It delivers few answers and, by itself, does not deliver predictability of decision. It has created difficult problems for application of traditional German methodology of legal norm and subsumption. Gerd Pfeiffer, president of the German Federal Supreme Court and chairman of its cartel senate, commented that indefinite legal concepts are the rule, and legal norms capable of immediate subsumption the exception in the GWB.[175] After nearly two decades as president of the Federal Cartel Authority, Eberhard Günther adjudged the GWB so filled with indefinite legal concepts that a "subsumption as traditionally known simply is not possible."[176]

This criticism recognizes that the GWB does not provide *the* right answer to a particular antitrust question. Instead the indefinite legal concepts force the decision maker to make policy decisions. He is not positively bound to one solution. Even though the GWB does not provide the answer, there is no uncertainty in antitrust law comparable to that in the United States. Nor is there a comparable dissatisfaction, even though to see legal certainty as an absolute value is said to be characteristic of the entire German civil law. Why then do even those critics particularly concerned with legal certainty nonetheless find the GWB tolerable or at least remediable without extensive changes?[177] The reason for this satisfaction can be read in the statute itself.

Although the GWB rarely delivers the definitive answer to an antitrust question, it does set the limits within which that answer is reached. The statute functions more as a control and a direction of decision, than as a determination of decision. In large measure, it has the character of a detailed set of instructions to an administrative agency.

The GWB brings certainty when it makes clear who is subject to a particular decision, when he is subject to it, what factors must be considered, and what the possible consequences of that decision are. The drafters of the GWB evidently thought that tightly drawn *Tatbestände* were likely to thwart the purposes of the law; consequently, an indefinite legal concept is apt to turn up in any given *Tatbestand*. But along with the indefinite legal concepts are also much more definite *Tatbestand* elements, which mark the limits of the norm. The GWB separates the various norms one from another through the use of different*Tatbestände*; it strives to insure that a particular factual situation falls under only one statutory provision.

One of the more successful limitations imposed by the GWB has been to clearly identify who is the addressee of a particular norm. Many of the GWB's major provisions apply only to enterprises. This requirement is generally considered to have been adopted specifically as a limit.[178] It keeps the household side of the economy from falling within these provisions: It thus rules out their application to consumers and laborers. Individuals controlling enterprises do not escape liability through this limitation, because they are still liable to administrative fines under piggyback provisions, when they are culpable. Another example of addressee limitation is the abuse control. Although the abuse control is very vague, only a few limited circles are subject to it: namely market dominating enterprises and particular parties that have received an exemption from GWB prohibitions.

The treatment of trade restraint by agreement is a good example of the separation of various *Tatbestände* in German cartel law. In American antitrust law a single prohibition of "contracts, combinations . . . , and conspiracies" covers a variety of agreements in restraint of trade, including even mergers. In German law, although the same agreements are covered, six different norms are used. Each brings its own conditions and limitations with it.[179]

Overall the GWB imposes fairly strong negative binding of antitrust decisions, even if the positive binding is rather weak. Some critics of the GWB encourage a more open acknowledgement of this fact. For example, Hans Hirsch recommends that greater efforts be made to draw firm lines around particular areas and that less attention be devoted to establishing a particular correct solution. He would then have the decision maker, even more than at present, be required to consider certain factors within that area of greater freedom.[180]

Perhaps the most important use of the German methodology of Norm = *Tatbestand* + legal consequence is the separate application of the various norms according to their legal consequences. The GWB appears to try to separate policy issues from equity issues; to separate future-oriented decisions from past-oriented ones. It accomplishes this division by limiting policy issues largely to consideration by an administrative authority and restricting legal consequences ordered by that authority in such policy decisions to future effect. This usage is discussed in the following chapter.

5

Separate Treatment of Equity and Policy Value Judgments

While specific *Tatbestand* elements, such as were discussed in Chapter 4, place important limits on policy decisions in German cartel law, perhaps the most important control is the indirect limit brought about by the organization of decision making. Where application of a particular norm requires freeing the decision maker from making a mere factual recognition and necessitates assigning him a more or less subjective value judgment, the GWB prefers administrative authorities for certain kinds of judgments and courts for others. The more a judgment requires an assessment of the general welfare, the more the GWB seeks to place the decision maker under a form of political responsibility. On the other hand, the more a judgment requires an equity determination, such as of individual culpability, the more the GWB seeks to distance the decision maker from any form of political control and to assure that he is responsible only to statute and justice (*Gesetz und Recht*). To implement this division of decision making, the GWB avoids mixing the two kinds of judgment in a single case. The device the GWB uses to effect this separation is the German methodology of norm and subsumption.

The GWB uses the relation between the two parts of the norm – the *Tatbestand* and the legal consequence – to separate certain kinds of equity issues (namely culpability) from policy issues. Ideally, all of the former are assigned to adjudication and all of the latter to administration. In the GWB future-oriented legal consequences are attached to norms which do not require judgments of culpability, while past-oriented legal consequences are attached to norms which do require such judgments. On the other hand, future-oriented legal consequences are often attached to norms which require policy judgments, while past-oriented legal consequences are rarely, if ever, attached to norms requiring such judgments. Here is the indirect limitation on antitrust policy decisions created by the system of organization: Policy judgments can almost always have only future effect. In American antitrust law there is no comparable separation of equity and policy judgments. Both kinds of judgment may be required in the same case. Questions of culpability often play a major role in future-oriented decisions; important policy decisions often have serious consequences for activity concluded in the past. This mixing of equity and policy judgments tends to reduce Rule of Law security and hamper wise policy decisions. Moreover, the relative effects of this mixing are magnified by the respective res judicata treatment of antitrust policy decisions in the two countries: In the United States antitrust policy decisions are judicial judgments and are therefore subject to the particularly strong form of res judicata which prevails here; in the Federal Republic of Germany, antitrust policy decisions are administrative decisions, and are therefore not subject to even the weak form of res judicata which prevails there.

THE SEPARATE TREATMENT OF THE DIFFERENT TYPES OF VALUE JUDGMENTS IN GERMAN CARTEL LAW BY THE SEPARATE APPLICATION OF NORMS ACCORDING TO THEIR LEGAL CONSEQUENCES

The German cartel law is not a listing of prohibitions with legal consequences in the fashion of many criminal codes and other comparable listings in the form: If A does X, A shall be imprisoned six months. Rather the GWB creates a system of interdependent partial norms which, when put together, form complete norms. These complete norms are of three broad types when categorized by the type of legal consequences they bring: prohibition norms, intervention norms, and permission norms. Prohibition norms (*Verbotsnormen*) prohibit certain conduct or conditions. These norms are the heart of the GWB. Of all the norms, they alone work by their being an actual change in legal relations; they alone can have a retrospective effect from the time of a decision applying them; and only they permit civil damages and quasi-criminal penalties. Intervention norms (*Eingriffsnormen*) do not effect a change in legal relationships, but confer a power to command a change in legal relationships. Usually this change takes the form of a prohibition of conduct or of an economic condition, but exceptionally it has the form of a positive direction of conduct. Permission norms (*Zulassungsnormen*) create a power to negate a prohibition. These three groups of norms interlock. A permission norm creates a power to negate a prohibition norm. An order prohibiting conduct pursuant to the power provided by an intervention norm may itself become the basis of a prohibition norm or, occasionally, of a permission norm. A permission norm, when exercised, often brings into being an intervention norm.

A value judgment in the application of a complete norm (as distinguished from the ascertainment of the applicable norm itself) can be lodged in two places: on the *Tatbestand* side or on the legal consequence side of the norm. As pointed out in Chapter 4, German law generally prefers limiting discretion to the legal consequence side; judgments on the *Tatbestand* side should not permit a choice of conclusions, but should acknowledge the possibility of only one right answer, however difficult reaching that answer may be.[181]

The GWB concentrates discretionary decisions (from the legal consequence side) as well as policy judgments (from the *Tatbestand* side) in the intervention and the permission norms. These norms are applied exclusively by administrative authorities. The GWB attempts to avoid discretion and policy judgments in the application of the prohibition norms. These are often applied by courts. In application of the prohibition norms the GWB distinguishes between the objective legal order and subjective legal consequences. Some of the prohibition norms of the GWB might be termed "base norms." They are complete norms in the sense that they bring objective changes in the legal order (for example, contract invalidity); at the same time they are partial norms which can be combined with other partial norms to create complete norms which support subjective legal consequences such as compensatory damages and quasi-criminal fines. The GWB always requires culpability as a prerequisite for subjective legal consequences such as civil damages and quasi-criminal penalties, but never requires culpability for the realization of objective consequences. The vehicle the GWB uses to effect these separations is the methodology of norm and subsumption.

As already shown, in German theory of legal method a complete norm consists of a *Tatbestand* and a legal consequence. Whenever a given *Tatbestand* is realized in a particular factual situation (*Sachverhalt*), then the corresponding legal consequence of that norm applies (*gilt*) to that factual situation. That legal consequence may be nothing more than creation of a power to make a discretionary choice of particular legal consequences. Looked at another way, a particular legal consequence can be applied to a particular factual situation *if and only if* the factual situation fulfills a particular *Tatbestand* directing (or permitting a discretionary choice of) that particular legal consequence. Each potential legal consequence is therefore connected to a particular *Tatbestand*: realization of the *Tatbestand* necessarily brings the legal consequence – the legal consequence cannot apply without realization of the *Tatbestand*.

Permission Norms

The permission norms require the most explicit general welfare judgments in German cartel law; they often require economic and other policy judgments. They empower administrative authorities to authorize cartel and other contracts which would otherwise violate statutory and other prohibitions. They can effect only the future. Permission norms empower administrative authorities to negate three different prohibitions: the general prohibition of cartel agreements of section 1 (subject to negation pursuant to sections 2-8); the specific prohibition of certain agreements concerning patents and similar rights of sections 20 and 21 (subject to negation pursuant to section 20 II); and, a merger prohibition issued by the Federal Cartel Authority pursuant to section 24 II (subject to negation pursuant to section 24 III).

The permission norms are of three types. A very few permit cartel agreements to become effective by the simple act of registering the agreement (*Anmeldungskartelle*).[182] When these norms apply, the power to negate the statutory prohibition rests with the parties to the agreement. Application of these permission norms does not require significant economic or other policy judgments. A more important group of permission norms allows negation of the section 1 cartel prohibition, provided certain documentation is filed with the cartel authorities, and provided the cartel authorities do not within a certain time (usually three months) object (so-called "*Widerspruchskartelle*").[183] The last major group, which encompasses the remaining negations of the cartel prohibition of section 1, as well as the negations affecting the prohibitions of certain patent agreements of section 20 and of mergers of section 23, requires a positive grant of permission. Sometimes the authorities have discretion whether to grant this permission (*Erlaubniskartelle ohne Anspruch*); other times the authorities have no discretion and the concerned parties have a right to have the permission issued (*Erlaubniskartelle mit Anspruch*).[184]

Permission norms which require positive grants of permission require the most overt and least specifically normed economic and general welfare judgments in German cartel law. The GWB assigns the two farthest-reaching such judgments to the minister for economics himself. Under section 8, if a cartel agreement is not otherwise eligible for permission, the minister for economics has discretion to permit such an agreement, where "in an exceptional case the restriction on competition is necessary for more important reasons of the entire economy and the public interest." Under section 24 III, the minister must authorize a merger which the Federal Cartel Authority has prohibited, "if in the particular case the restriction on competition is offset by advantages for the economy generally resulting from the merger or the merger is justified by an overriding public interest," provided that "the free market economy is not endangered by the extent of the restriction on competition." Other permission norms assign explicit economic and other policy decisions to the administrative authorities. For example, section 4 gives the Federal Cartel Authority discretion to authorize structural crisis cartels in certain limited instances, when necessary "to bring about a systematic adjustment of capacity to demand, and the arrangement is reached with due regard for the economy generally and for the general welfare."[185] Although generally the discretion granted decision makers in the GWB is subject to an unusually wide ranging judicial review, section 70 withdraws from review "the assessment of the general economic situation and development," in order, presumably, to assure political responsibility for these decisions.[186]

These and other permission norms also require more specific economic or other policy judgments, such as, whether a potential cartel agreement will serve "to improve satisfaction of demand" (§ 5 II), or whether a cartel agreement will "permit substantial competition in the market to continue" (§ 5a I). Sometimes, the cartel authorities must make findings, such as that "the rationalization is desirable for the public interest" (§ 5 III), or that "the interest in maintaining competition predominates" (§ 6 III).

When the GWB empowers the minister or the cartel authorities to authorize an otherwise prohibited agreement or merger, almost always it bestows discretion to issue the permission subject to "restrictions, conditions and requirements" (*Beschränkungen, Bedingungen und Auflagen*: § 11 III for cartels), or to "restrictions and requirements" (*Beschränkungen und Auflagen*: § 24 III for mergers).[187] Once cartels are authorized pursuant to one of these norms, the GWB gives the cartel authorities discretion to rescind that permission later, should the determinative conditions for the authorization change or if the requirements imposed have not been fulfilled (§ 11 IV). As a rule, the cartel authorities may not grant a permission valid for more than three years (§ 11 I).[188]

All of the permission norms, which allow cartel agreements otherwise invalid under section 1, lead to the creation of intervention norms. These intervention norms are of two types. Where the cartel authorities have negated the statutory prohibition by the explicit grant of a permission, section 11 V *requires* them to intervene and to withdraw or to modify the permission, whenever one of several conditions is met; the most important of these conditions is the abuse of the position of freedom afforded by the permission. On the other hand, where the cartel is effective upon registration *(Anmeldungskartelle)* or upon registration without subsequent objection (*Widerspruchskartelle*), section 12 gives the cartel authorities discretionary power to intervene and to order one of several measures, whenever one of two conditions is met. Almost always, one of these conditions is the abuse of the freedom granted.[189] Presumably, the cartel authorities are not required to intervene in the latter case, because these cartels are thought to provide less of a threat to competition and to the general welfare.

Intervention Norms

While permission norms specify cases where general welfare considerations demand relaxing a general rule of prohibition, intervention norms specify cases where general welfare considerations demand limitation of a general rule of freedom. The intervention norms grant the cartel authorities a power, usually discretionary,[190] to issue one of a number of prohibitions, or, in a few peculiar instances, to issue positive commands.[191]

The previous subsection considered the most important of those intervention norms which exist to supervise freedom granted from general prohibition norms.[192] Besides this type of abuse control, there are three other major types of intervention norms: controls of market power, controls on development of market power, and controls of certain noncartel contracts. The controls of market power are two. Section 22 V grants the cartel authorities discretionary powers to prohibit conduct and declare contracts ineffective, whenever a market dominating enterprise engages in abusive conduct. Before they may issue an order pursuant to this section, the cartel authorities must, as a rule (*soll* provision), request that the enterprise concerned discontinue the conduct. Section 37a III grants the cartel authorities a discretionary power to prohibit conduct by an enterprise which has a superior position, as against smaller-sized competitors, when the conduct "inequitably hinders these competitors directly or indirectly, and is likely to have a lasting effect on competition."[193] The latter provision was adopted only in 1980. The merger control of German cartel law is also embodied in an intervention norm. Section 24 I gives the Federal Cartel Authority a power, which it must exercise, to prohibit any merger that would result in or strengthen a market-dominating position. Section 24 takes away that power if the affected enterprises prove "that because of the merger improvements in competitive conditions will also occur and that these improvements outweigh the disadvantages of the market domination." Finally, section 18 grants the cartel authorities discretionary powers to declare certain abusive noncartel contracts (mostly supplier/customer contracts) ineffective from the date of the order or from some future time and to prohibit further use of such contracts.

The intervention norms share certain general characteristics. The powers the intervention norms grant are all negative: They are powers to create prohibitions similar to those of the prohibition norms. With the few exceptions already mentioned, the exercise of those powers is discretionary.

Application of the intervention norms therefore forces the decision maker to make policy judgments on both *Tatbestand* and legal consequence sides of the norm. On the *Tatbestand* side the decision maker must make many economic decisions. For example, he may be required to decide whether an enterprise is subject to the norm, because it is market dominating or because a merger would make it market dominating.[194] He may then be required to decide whether conduct is abusive. The GWB itself does not much limit these determinations through helping norms. It does provide general directions to the decision maker to help him determine whether there is market domination, by providing certain presumptions of market dominance (§ 22 I-III). The GWB also gives examples of abuses of market-dominating positions from which the decision maker may proceed by analogy to adjudge particular conduct (§ 22 IV). Determination of whether there is a market-dominating position and whether it has been abused necessarily involves the decision maker in the determination of a relevant market and of the enterprise's strength in that market. If, and only if, the decision maker determines that the particular enterprise satisfies the preconditions of the appropriate *Tatbestand*, can he then make the second policy judgment, and determine, in his discretion which, if any, of the potential legal consequences he is authorized to impose, he will apply. Policy judgments on both sides of the norm are thus inescapable. Their effect, however, is limited to the future.[195]

Prohibition Norms

So far this chapter has considered norms that have legal consequences with only future effects: The permission norms permit the negation of a prohibition and the intervention norms create powers to impose prohibitions. While the former require party petition, the latter ordinarily do not, but both are implemented primarily by administrative action without recourse to the ordinary courts (except in a reviewing function). These norms frequently require policy judgments for application; they never require judgments of individual culpability. In all these respects, the prohibition norms differ, at least in the usual course, and subject to qualifications discussed in the immediately following subsection.

The prohibition norms are constructed from a base norm and from helping norms. The base norm makes an objective change in the legal order. These base norms are of two types: statutory prohibitions and administrative prohibitions ordered pursuant to intervention norms. Both types appear as prohibitions of conduct and as prohibitions of certain contracts (resulting in contract unenforceability or voidness). Contracts subject to prohibitions include cartel agreements (§ 1), vertical price maintenance contracts (§ 15), and certain contracts affecting patent and similar rights (§§ 20, 21). Conduct subject to statutory prohibitions includes interdependent conduct which could not be subject to a valid agreement under the GWB (§ 25 I), threats to compel engagement in such conduct (§ 25 II), boycotts of certain types (§ 26), and recommendations to engage in conduct violating prohibitions of the law (§ 38 I No. 11). The previous subsection already touched upon the corresponding prohibitions that can be issued pursuant to the intervention norms.

The statutory base norms do not generally require extensive economic judgments for their application. Compared to the intervention norms and to the permission norms, they require relatively few, if any, policy judgments in their application. They do not explicitly require judgments of the general welfare or of a particular effect on competition. With rare exception, these base norms do not require resort to extensive market analysis; only one statutory prohibition requires the decision maker even to draw a relevant market. Still greater specificity should be expected from prohibitions issued pursuant to intervention norms. Though there are some imperfections to this scheme which are discussed in the immediately following subsection, the clear goal is to maximize certainty and eliminate policy judgments in the application of the prohibition norms.

Although avoiding policy judgments in their application, prohibition norms do require additional equity decisions before they permit imposing civil damages or quasi-criminal fines. These additional decisions serve to insure that compensation is required only for a superior claim of legal right and punishment is imposed only for a clearly defined legal wrong. Prohibition norms do not require these additional equity decisions for less repressive legal consequences such as contract invalidity.

Civil Law Consequences

Some base norms can be enforced as prohibition norms without more. Private parties may raise the contract prohibitions as defenses to enforcement of otherwise apparently valid contracts. Section 37a I-II gives the cartel authorities discretionary power to forbid execution of contracts unenforceable under the GWB and to prohibit conduct violating prohibition norms. Besides direct enforcement, base norms can be enforced as parts of other prohibition norms, which authorize private actions (for injunctions or for damages) or quasi-criminal prosecutions.

Private parties may bring suit in the ordinary courts to enforce base norms, whenever the statutory prohibition or the order of the cartel authority "has as its purpose the protection of another person" (§ 35 I). The requirement of a protective character corresponds to the general rule of German tort law.[196] A statute or order has protective character, if it is a command or prohibition (*Gebot* or *Verbot*), and if it has as its primary purpose the protection of individuals or groups (even if at the same time serving the protection of the community).[197] The question of protective character must be determined for each individual case; the answer is often hotly disputed. If the statute or order meets this requirement, then the private party is entitled to an injunction (*Unterlassung*), which prohibits carrying out the contract or conduct. If, in addition, the private party has suffered damages, and if the defendant was at fault, the private party is also entitled to civil damages. This entitlement arises from a separate prohibition norm. The requirement that the defendant be at fault corresponds to the general rule of German tort law that an actor is liable for damages only if he has acted culpably, or if, exceptionally, a statute makes him liable for the fault of another.[198]

Quasi-Criminal Sanctions

Base norms can also be enforced as parts of quasi-criminal norms, known as *Ordnungswidrigkeiten* or regulatory infractions. The concept of regulatory infractions is a German invention of this century; it seeks to separate reproachable infractions of policy and administrative order from criminal acts as such. The fine for a regulatory infraction is known as a *Bußgeld* or penalty rather than as a *Geldstrafe* or fine. The purpose of the penalty is "not to 'atone' for a deed [or] to bring about expiation for social-ethical culpability; rather, in the first instance, it is directed toward enforcing a particular order."[199] The GWB permits a penalty up to 1 million DM and, over and above that, threefold the excess profits (*Mehrerlös*) achieved by the illegal behavior (§ 38 IV).

Because of its close connection to criminal law, the law of regulatory infractions is generally subject to the strict Rule of Law requirements of German criminal law. Above all, it is subject to the requirements of *nullum crimen, nulla poena, sine lege* and of culpability (*Schuldprinzip*). There are, however, important differences between the law of regulatory infractions and the criminal law, which are usually said to be justified either by the reduced repressive effect or by the greater administrative character of regulatory infractions. The principle of compulsory prosecution (*Legalitätsprinzip*) does not prevail in the law of regulatory infractions; instead a principle of discretionary prosecution (*Opportunitätsprinzip*) applies. The administrative authorities have discretion whether to prosecute regulatory infractions. The diminished repressive nature of the quasi-criminal penalty is not the only reason a relaxation of the criminal law requirements is acceptable in the law of regulatory infractions. More important are the protections provided by the procedures required of the administration, and the possibility of full judicial review. These other protections are particularly developed in cartel law. For example, in cartel law infractions an appellate court has the function normally assigned the lowest courts in the usual regulatory infractions. The justification usually given for the substitution of a rule of discretionary prosecution (*Opportunitätsprinzip*) for the more usual rule of compulsory prosecution is that in the areas assigned to regulatory infraction law, the legislature has less interest in how the administration maintains a particular order, than that it does. The administrative authorities are deliberately allowed freedom to decide what mix of repressive and nonrepressive measures should be used to maintain a particular order.[200]

The prohibitions of German cartel law – whether incorporated in statutory prohibition norms or issued by administrative authorities pursuant to intervention norms – are enforced as parts of regulatory infraction norms and can thus lead to the imposition of quasi-criminal penalties and forfeiture of excess profits. As all regulatory infraction norms do, these prohibition norms require proof of illegality (*Rechtswidrigkeit*) and culpability §§ 1, 10 OWiG.

The base norm of the GWB is not the (narrow) *Tatbestand*; the GWB provisions setting the regulatory infraction norm add additional elements to those of the base norm to form the *Tatbestand*. Where a contract has been forbidden by statute or by administrative order, the GWB requires the additional element of disregarding (*Hinwegsetzung*) the voidness or unenforceability of the contract (§ 38 I Nos. 1 & 2, respectively). With this requirement, the GWB assures that only the implementation of such a contract, and not the mere conclusion of it, can be sanctioned quasi-criminally.[201] Where conduct has been forbidden by statute or by administrative order, the only additional element the GWB requires is actual contrary action (*Zuwiderhandlung*) (§ 38 I No. 8). In cases of administrative prohibition of conduct, however, the GWB requires that the administrative order (*Verfügung*), which prohibits the conduct, make explicit reference to the possibility of a quasi-criminal penalty should there be noncompliance (§ 38 I Nos. 4-6). Since it is not incorporated in an administrative order (*Verfügung*), a request to discontinue conduct constituting an abuse of a market-dominating position (compare § 22 V) cannot, by itself, lead to a *Geldbuße*.

The regulatory infraction provisions of the German cartel law set different levels of culpability for the imposition of quasi-criminal penalties. Where the prohibition comes immediately from the GWB, the GWB requires that the violation be intentional (*vorsätzlich*) (§ 38 I Nos. 1, 8 with § 10 OWiG). Where the prohibition stems from an order of the cartel authorities, the GWB requires only that the violation be negligent (*fahrlässig*) § 38 I Nos. 2,4-6. Probably this difference is because the administrative order is already case-specific.

Illegality (*Rechtswidrigkeit*), which requires the absence of grounds for justification, has had some significance in determining whether certain conduct might have been authorized by other administrative order. However, Tiedemann points out that it does not introduce a rule of reason (so expressed by Tiedemann), which would allow argument that the conduct was justified for other societal reasons.[202]

Result of the Separate Treatment: Limitation of Policy Decisions to Legal Consequences Having Only Future Effect

How the GWB attempts to separate questions of policy from questions of culpability is apparent. Past-directed legal consequences, such as civil damages and quasi-criminal fines, always require proof of culpability; future-directed civil and administrative consequences do not. The GWB concentrates policy judgments in the intervention and permission norms; it avoids requiring them in the prohibition norms. Only the prohibition norms can lead directly to the past-directed consequences requiring culpability. In such cases, if there is a policy decision, it has been made already, either by statute or by administrative action, before these prohibition norms are brought into play.

Where concern is the future structure of the economy – with the general welfare – the GWB insures that the investigation avoids irrelevant issues of individual culpability and concentrates on the central question of economic or other effect upon the general welfare. The GWB protects the affected party, because it insures that he suffer nothing worse than abandonment of the challenged practice. On the other hand, where the GWB authorizes sanctioning the party concerned for a wrong, that wrong will already have been fairly clearly formulated in a statutory or administrative prohibition. The party need not act at his peril, experience a policy decision which determines that his challenged practice reduces competition, and then suffer the consequences of civil damages and criminal sanctions. Rule of Law security is enhanced.[203]

Imperfections in the Separate Treatment

Although the GWB has had considerable success in separating culpability judgments from policy decisions and in confining the effect of the latter to the future, there are imperfections. Here three such imperfections are considered, one of which arises out of the GWB itself, another out of court decisions, and a third out of administrative practice. To a certain extent, all three share the common characteristic that they are situations where there is a reduced general welfare interest and a correspondingly increased individual interest.

§ 26 II GWB

As a rule the GWB avoids the use of market analyses in application of prohibition norms. However, GWB section 26 II forces the decision maker to make a decision which evaluates competition. It prohibits discrimination and unjust hindering (*unbillige Behinderung*) in competition, if the actor is market dominating or in other ways has a certain market power. The GWB sanctions violations of section 26 II with damages and quasi-criminal penalties. In applying this provision, the decisive question in practice is whether a given actor is subject to the norm.[204] This question can be answered only after a judgment of the state of competition on a given market. As this provision has received broader application, it has been increasingly defended more for its protection of freedom and equality and less for its protection of competition. This section has been subject to substantial criticism on both grounds of economic policy and of Rule of Law security.[205]

Judicial Construction of § 1 GWB

Some legal decisions have tended toward introducing market analyses in application of prohibition norms. Section 1 of the GWB makes contracts and association decisions ineffective "insofar as they are likely through restraints on competition, to affect production or market conditions of commerce in goods or commercial services." The German Federal Supreme Court has held that this requirement that the contract be suited to restrict competition requires that an effect on competition be perceivable (*spürbar*).[206] In the middle 1970s the Court went a step further and held that this judgment requires drawing a relevant market.[207] Critics of this construction argued that the statutory requirement serves only to assure that there is some effect on competition, but that the magnitude of the effect is unimportant.[208] In that case, any economic judgment would be very simple, if necessary at all.

It may be that the suitability requirement was added for equity considerations. If the restriction is not suited to restrict competition, the general welfare interest recedes and doubts can be resolved in favor of the market participant. In any case, the Court has adhered to its position despite the criticism. So far the lower courts have not used this requirement to take on a major policy role and there has been little serious concern about the Court's adherence to its position.[209]

Application of § 1 GWB by the Administrative Authorities

Administrative practice has sought similarly to restrict the reach of section 1, where the interest in competition recedes and the interest of the individual comes to the forefront. The Federal Ministry for Economics has issued detailed interpretative guidelines which clarify when a joint venture is subject to scrutiny under the GWB. They state certain forms of intercorporate cooperation are not to be considered violations of section 1.[210] The Federal Cartel Authority has also detailed its enforcement policy with respect to the exercise of its discretion to prosecute potential violations. Particularly noteworthy in this regard is its policy with respect to "bagatelle" cartels, cartels having a particularly small market share (less than 5 percent), and not acting on central economic decisions such as price are ignored.[211] In such cases, the contract is still contrary to law (*rechtswidrig*) and cannot be enforced. Since the broadening of the possibilities for the permission of such cartels pursuant to section 5b, the utility of such a limited construction of section 1 has been questioned.[212] Still, this administrative practice may not be an especially serious imperfection in the separation of difficult economic questions from past-oriented implementation. In either case (as the Ministry notes in its guidelines), an enterprise with doubts as to legality may always file a formal application for a cartel permission with the cartel authorities. Moreover, the Federal Cartel Authority informally reviews "bagatelle" cartels upon request.[213] But at least to an extent, these imperfections do throw Rule of Law security even in past-oriented enforcement back to administrative policy. Where the administrative policy changes, or where a private litigant may sue, possible unpleasant surprises cannot be foreclosed.[214] On the other hand, to the extent those policy decisions are strictly limited to formal policy statements, the goal of eliminating policy decisions from the individual case may be fulfilled.[215]

Disadvantages of the Separate Treatment

What costs do others bear as a result of the attempted separation of policy and equity questions in the implementation of the law? Often third parties are protected in their participation in the market by the GWB; do they suffer from the separation? In the case of the permission practice, it seems not; they may even benefit. Applications for cartel permissions receive publicity, are subject to publication and to public comment. Sometimes the GWB specifically requires the cartel authority to consider specific third parties, even to the extent of requiring the applicant to solicit their comments as part of the application itself. On the other hand, in the case of the intervention norms, third parties are probably somewhat disadvantaged by limitation of policy decisions to future effect. Under intervention norms, a practice is permitted until prohibited. Third parties are therefore remedyless until a cartel authority intervenes.[216] While they may petition for an investigation and in certain cases can compel one, whatever damages arise until an intervention order is issued go uncompensated. This problem has been recognized. Recently there was a proposal that private parties be assured a right of action for damages for abuse of a market-dominating position, even in the absence of an administrative order. This proposal was rejected; it would have been inconsistent with the separation of economic policy decisions from past-oriented enforcement. Nevertheless, a compromise interesting from the standpoint of Rule of Law security was reached. An excess profit achieved through an abuse of a market-dominating position is subject to forfeiture; that forfeiture relates back to the time of the initial intervention of the cartel authority, and not just to when the order became final (§ 37b I 1).[217]

THE ABSENCE OF A SEPARATION OF POLICY AND EQUITY JUDGMENTS IN AMERICAN ANTITRUST LAW

American antitrust law does not separate equity from policy judgments. Frequently both equity and policy judgments are reached in one and the same case by one and the same decision maker.[218] American antitrust law does not tie a particular legal consequence to a specific substantive requirement. Instead, it furnishes a pool of substantive requirements and a pool of legal consequences which largely can be freely attached one to the other. The requirements it imposes for invoking one legal consequence are largely the same as for any other. Because of the res judicata effect of an antitrust judgment, to assign one legal consequence can be to assign them all. Thus it is difficult, or even impossible, to limit legal consequences to a future effect.[219] Indeed, the system of common law remedies and statutory requirements tends to prefer the past-directed legal consequences, and thus further complicates a distinction between equity and policy judgments.

Criminal Law Sanctions

American antitrust law is a law of wrongs. Its substantive provisions consist solely of prohibitions. Antitrust decisions therefore always determine rights and duties. But, as shown in Chapter 3, American antitrust decisions often require policy judgments. Under the Sherman Act the policy judgment is an application of the Rule of Reason; under the Clayton Act the policy judgment is a determination of an effect which "may be substantially to lessen competition or tend to create a monopoly." Once this judgment is made, a plethora of undifferentiated remedies becomes available.

American law offers a wide variety of civil and criminal consequences. It sets largely the same requirements for all consequences, whether future or past directed, whether nonrepressive or repressive. It permits ordering any civil law consequences for violation of any of the major substantive provisions of the Sherman and Clayton Acts. It does, however, limit criminal law consequences to violations of the Sherman Act. While American antitrust law permits an array of public and private enforcers to invoke civil sanctions, it allows only the Department of Justice to seek criminal sanctions.

Section 1 of the Sherman Act makes concluding a contract in restraint of trade punishable. The mere entering into agreement is sufficient; carrying out the contract or conspiracy has been thought unnecessary under the Sherman Act. Section 2 of the Sherman Act makes attempt to monopolize punishable. The courts have held that intent to monopolize is an element of monopolization, whether prosecuted civilly or criminally.[220]

The Antitrust Division of the Department of Justice controls criminal law enforcement of the Sherman Act.[221] The Attorney General has discretion whether to initiate a criminal prosecution. Under long-standing practices, the Department of Justice has restricted criminal enforcement to clear violations of per se rules;[222] it avoids bringing criminal prosecutions when a policy judgment would be necessary in the application of the law. As is typical of American criminal law generally, the Antitrust Division can agree with the defendant that the defendant will plead guilty or nolo contendere in exchange for the prosecution's recommendation of sentence or for other consideration.[223] In that event, there is no trial and no judicial decision, although there is a judgment ("consent judgment"). By entering a nolo contendere plea, the defendant avoids res judicata effects, which could lead to other civil law consequences.

Civil Law Consequences

While American antitrust law limits criminal law consequences to violations of the Sherman Act, it applies civil law consequences to all violations of the major provisions of the Sherman and Clayton Acts alike. These civil law consequences fall into two broad categories: damages and injunctions.

Practically anyone can seek damages for practically any violation of the antitrust laws: namely, according to section 4 of the Clayton Act, "Any person who shall be injured in his business or property by reason of anything forbidden in the antitrust laws."[224] The successful plaintiff recovers, according to the same provision, three times the damages he proves; the trial judge has no discretion to reduce this amount. The courts have vacillated in how they view the repressive character of treble damages. Sometimes they seem prepared to acknowledge the repressive – criminal law-like – character of three-fold damages, while other times they prefer to see a purely remedial character.[225] In order to invoke the treble damages remedy, the private plaintiff must show violation of the antitrust laws and an injury to his business or property. The Supreme Court has held that "Plaintiffs must prove antitrust injury, which is to say injury of the type the antitrust laws were intended to prevent and that flows from that which makes defendants' acts unlawful."[226] Lately, this requirement has become a focal point of efforts to limit treble damages.[227]

Under section 4C(a) (1), an attorney general of any one of the 50 constituent states of the American union may sue for treble damages on behalf of "natural persons residing in such state . . . for injury sustained by such natural persons to their property by reason of any violation of the Sherman Act." This is called a "parens patriae action" and is not available for Clayton Act violations. The attorneys general are officials of the state and are completely independent of the federal Department of Justice; they are usually elected. Under section 4A of the Clayton Act, the government of the United States may sue for single damages for violations of both the Clayton and the Sherman Acts, whenever it is "injured in its business or property."

Almost as many parties in almost as many instances may sue for injunctions as may sue for damages. The U.S. Attorney General is authorized to seek injunctions to "prevent and restrain violations" of the Sherman and Clayton Acts. Private parties are authorized "to sue for and have injunctive relief . . . as against threatened loss or damage by a violation of the antitrust laws" (§ 16 Clayton Act). Moreover, the Federal Trade Commission may issue an injunction-like "cease and desist" order, when it can characterize the antitrust violation as an unfair trade practice (§ 5 FTC Act).

As with criminal enforcement of the Sherman Act, government civil enforcement of the antitrust laws is centered with the Antitrust Division of the Department of Justice, though here the FTC also plays a significant role. Again, as with criminal enforcement, the government authorities may reach an agreement with the defendant, which avoids trial and the res judicata effects of an antitrust judgment (consent judgment, or if with the FTC, consent order). A consent judgment is a judicial judgment which, since 1974, has been subject to court review. The reviewing court must find that the entry of the judgment is "in the public interest" (§ 5(e) Clayton Act).[228]

The injunction has many forms. It may be a simple, general prohibition: Do not violate the antitrust laws. It may be a specific prohibition: Do not restrict your distribution to particular territories. Or the injunction may be a positive command: Sell assets, lease property, license patents, share expertise, or, even, finance a new competitor. Neither statute nor judicial precedent limits the scope of injunctions.[229]

Judicial principles do guide application of injunctions. An injunction should be broad enough that it remedies the violation, or prevents the injury; but it should not be so broad as to be punitive.[230] While the injunction can have practically unlimited scope, it does not have completely unlimited availability. The most important limit on injunctions stems from the self-imposed limitation of the English Court of Equity, which held that it would not issue an injunction when a common law court could order an adequate remedy. In the American systems which have merged law and equity courts this limit has the form of the maxim: equitable relief should be ordered only when the remedy at law (usually damages) is inadequate.[231] This limit encourages litigants to seek money damages rather than injunctions.

III Effects for Rule of Law Security and for Policy of Mixing Equity and Policy Judgments

The different sanctions for violation of the American antitrust law are scarcely differentiated by different elements. Most antitrust law violations can potentially be sanctioned by criminal punishments, treble damages, and equity injunctions. Because of the effect of res judicata (discussed in the next section), even when only one type of sanction is sought in a particular case, the other sanctions cannot be forgotten. Although in a particular case the judge may be asked only to issue an injunction, some other party may later utilize that finding to support a claim for treble damages. Thus, in every antitrust case, the treble damages sanction is an omnipresent possibility.[232]

Some legal consequences of U.S. antitrust law, such as treble damages and criminal punishment, are highly repressive. To order such repressive sanctions in the absence of culpability would be contrary to American traditions of justice. Because treble damages are an omnipresent possibility, the judge, who is interested in fairness, will in every case look for evidence of the defendant's culpability; he will look for the fault which confirms the breach of duty. For the same reason, the judge will look for evidence of injury. The judge will wish to hold the defendant responsible only for the injury he has caused.[233]

This search for injury is encouraged in private cases by the rule that an injunction is proper only if the remedy at law (damages) is inadequate. Before the judge can know if money is an adequate remedy, he must know what the damage is. When the judge orders an injunction, he will determine the scope of the injunction by resorting to past-directed measures – the extent of the injury (if the injunction is sought by a private party claiming injury) or by the extent of the violation (if the injunction is sought by the government claiming violations of law).[234]

This search for culpability and harm is not startling; an analogous search is made in German cartel law whenever repressive sanctions are ordered pursuant to prohibition norms.[235] What is startling is that in American law a policy decision may be distorted by this search for culpability and injury. Because German law separates equity and policy decisions, the two decisions are not intermixed. When a policy decision is made, general welfare is the measure of decision. General welfare has little concern for individual culpability or individual harm. If general welfare is the interest protected, there may be no "victims" who individually suffered injury. Dollar damages resulting from proscribed conduct may be elusive, impossible to estimate, or enormous. Because the sanction system directs attention to the past, the judge may have to choose between fairness to the defendant and wisdom in his policy decision. If general welfare is at stake, the future is more important than the past. The judge will serve that interest better if he orders a future-oriented modification of the challenged practice than if he makes a past-oriented determination of wrong. Under present American law a policy decision may turn on a question of individual harm or culpability.

ANTITRUST POLICY JUDGMENTS AS ADMINISTRATIVE ACTS OR AS JUDICIAL JUDGMENTS

In both the United States and the Federal Republic of Germany judicial procedure usually leads to a judgment; German administrative procedure, on the other hand, usually leads to an "administrative act" (*Verwaltungsakt*). Because American antitrust law is applied by courts, its policy decisions are incorporated in judgments. Because German cartel law is applied by both courts and administrative authorities, its policy decisions do not have to be incorporated in judgments; they can be, and mostly are, incorporated in administrative acts.

Ordinarily a judicial judgment resolves a conflict about disputed claims of right. Although the German administrative act is like a judgment in that it is a mandatory disposition of an individual case, it only exceptionally, and then only provisionally, resolves a conflict in a given factual situation.[236] Judicial procedure serves not only to resolve disputed claims of right justly, but also to end conflict and to bring peace. Peace demands end to conflict, without regard to the justice of the conflict resolution.[237] Because of this interest in peace, judges are obligated to reach a decision. That decision, once embodied in a judgment, and after all appeals have been exhausted, is final; barring extraordinary circumstances, it cannot be challenged. This decision is a final determination of right. In part for that reason, judges are guaranteed independence.

General welfare decisions by their nature can rarely be final. While individuals have limited life, the community continues indefinitely. Conditions change. The community changes. Ideas change. What is the general welfare of the community changes? A legal system that denies itself the flexibility to change general welfare decisions cannot long avoid strains. The German cartel law brings flexibility to general welfare decisions through use of the administrative act. Strains result in American antitrust law because of the exclusive reliance on judicial judgments. To be sure, American antitrust law attempts to bring flexibility to judicial judgments, but that flexibility is within the context of a determination of conflicting claims of right. Flexibility must directly battle the traditional Rule of Law security interests of judgments; as a result, wise policy decisions may sometimes be bought only at the cost of legal certainty.

Res Judicata and Policy

Both German and American law incorporate principles that a controversy once judicially resolved should not be relitigated. The res judicata doctrine of the common law is, however, considerably broader than its German counterpart, *materielle Rechtskraft*. Res judicata does not merely bar a second action on the same claim between the same parties. Through the doctrine of collateral estoppel (issue preclusion), it can give a prior judgment a res judicata effect for different claims and for different parties than were involved in the original suit. If a particular issue was litigated by a party and was necessarily determined by the court, res judicata gives effect to the prior determination of that issue even though the cause of action is entirely different, and sometimes, even when nonparties to the original lawsuit are involved.[238] Ordinarily, collateral estoppel will not apply, if a party against whom it is raised had a full, fair, and ample opportunity to litigate that issue in the prior forum.[239] The German doctrine of res judicata (*materielle Rechtskraft*) does not have issue preclusion effect. It applies only between the parties to the prior suit and to their successors. It relates only to that claim (*Streitgegenstand*).[240]

Fundamentally, all American antitrust judgments have full res judicata effect (including issue preclusion).[241] In contrast, only some German antitrust decisions have res judicata effect; namely, court judgments and administrative fines. Otherwise, the general rule of German administrative law applies: An administrative act, in the absence of specific provision to the contrary, does not have res judicata effect.[242] Because an administrative act does not have res judicata effect, ordinarily it may be altered or revoked relatively easily.

Although German cartel law has three kinds of norms (prohibition, intervention, and permission), only the application of prohibition norms leads to decisions having res judicata effect. Of the four sanctions for prohibition norms, all but one have res judicata effect. Court judgments assigning damages, court judgments determining civil law consequences such as contractual invalidity, and cartel authority decisions ordering quasi-criminal fines all have res judicata effect. Only a cartel authority cease and desist order (*Untersagung*) does not enjoy *materielle Rechtskraft*. On the other hand, the application of intervention and permission norms does not lead to decisions having res judicata effect, even when challenged before the courts. Accordingly, merger decisions, cartel authorizations, and orders prohibiting abuses of market-dominating positions do not have res judicata effect.

In American law, practically all antitrust judgments have res judicata effect.[243] Judgments for damages and for criminal punishment become final and cannot be altered. Unless a device such as the nolo contendere plea is utilized to reduce the res judicata effect,[244] issue preclusion applies with full force.[245]

Equity decrees permit somewhat more flexibility. They also have full res judicata effect (including issue preclusion), but while the determination of right stands, a party may petition the court to modify the decree's remedies to take into account changed circumstances. This process is not simple and may require almost a whole new action. The original decree becomes a bit of law in itself, whose meaning the antitrust authorities cannot "unilaterally change."[246] The procedure by which an equity decree is altered retains the adversary character of the original litigation. This can militate against modification of the original decree. A change that a defendent views as more burdensome he will attack as an impermissible expansion of the original decree. Normally, such a later expansion of the earlier decree has little chance of success if it was not specifically reserved as a possibility under the original decree. That being so, the other side, private or public, may likewise be unwilling to relinquish its hard won "gains."[247]

The duty of decision, like the judgment, pushes American antitrust law toward a final decision and makes temporizing difficult. In almost all controversies subject to judicial resolution, the judge is subject to a duty of decision. Thus, in antitrust law a judge is forced to determine the permissibility of a particular practice as soon as a controversy is brought to him. There is neither an internal nor an external control over which cases are submitted for decision. To the contrary, the general clauses of the antitrust laws encourage litigants to raise all manner of questions. Then the judge has to decide whether the challenged conduct is legal, and often must make an economic judgment of the effect of the conduct. Moreover, his judgment is final: it has res judicata effect between the parties and is a precedent for everyone.[248]

The duty of decision is much weaker in German cartel law than it is in its American counterpart. Other than in application of prohibition norms in civil procedure, a duty of decision either does not exist or is weak. The general rule of German administrative law is that ordinarily, where there is no explicit requirement that the administration take action, and where there is no explicit right granted a third to apply for administrative action, the administrative agency has discretion whether to conduct an administrative inquiry.[249] Thus, in the usual case the administrative agency is not required to reach a decision whether the substantive norm could apply in the particular case. Consequently, only exceptionally is application of a GWB intervention or permission norm subject to a duty of decision. GWB permission norms create a duty of decision when they bestow a right to apply for exemption. But then the decision required is always tentative and never permanent. For example, as a rule a permission may not be granted for a period longer than three years.

The finality of the judicial judgment and the duty of judicial decision bring a degree of inflexibility to American antitrust law which works against wise policy. Comparable requirements of finality and decision are not found on the administrative side of the German cartel law, where policy decisions are concentrated. The use of the administrative act permits an easier trial and error application of the German cartel law than is possible in American antitrust law. An American court must uphold or prohibit a cartel agreement for all time. Because its judgment is final, an American court may waffle in order to bring flexibility to its decision: It may avoid decision altogether, or in some other way try to make its decision tentative, for example, by making its judgment indefinite or closely limited to particular facts. Legal certainty suffers. In Germany the comparable question is ordinarily a question of cartel permission. If the cartel authority allows the cartel, it authorizes the cartel for only a limited time and may impose restrictions. The tentative character of the policy decision is expressly recognized; these policy decisions are made tentatively and legal certainty need not suffer. Similarly, in control of powerful enterprises, the American court may be forced to decide forever an attempted monopolization case, where the German cartel authority can take a wait-and-see approach or may adopt a trial solution. Moreover, because the American antitrust decision is final and has a strong and largely unforeseeable res judicata effect, the parties are forced to fight hard for their views.

Res Judicata and Rule of Law Security

The freedom the lack of res judicata effect permits the cartel authorities raises Rule of Law security problems. When, and to what extent, may one rely on prior action or inaction of the cartel authorities? Of course, this is a problem for administrative law generally, and German administrative law has attempted to deal with it where administrative action takes the form of an administrative act. The general rule is that a nonbenefiting (*nicht begünstigender*) administrative act ordinarily may be freely withdrawn or altered with effect for the future (ex nunc). A benefiting administrative act, on the other hand, may be withdrawn or altered with future effect only if one of several particular grounds is met. While these provisions permit a freer alteration than is possible for judicial judgments, they are still restrictive. The benefiting administrative act is held to give rise to a reliance interest (*Vertrauensschutz*) on the part of the beneficiary. Recent litigation has raised the questions whether these general principles apply to the GWB, and when past administrative action creates a reliance interest.

These questions have arisen in the course of application of prohibition and permission norms.[250] In one case, the Federal Cartel Authority changed its position whether a particular contractual clause violated the prohibition of GWB § 15. The German Federal Supreme Court ruled that the Federal Cartel Authority's prior inaction, even though explicitly incorporated in an official policy statement, could not create a reliance interest. The Court held that an illegal contract term could not be legalized by administrative action, and therefore a nonprosecution policy could not create a reliance interest.[251] In the second situation, raised in two different cases, the Supreme Court considered instances where the Federal Cartel Authority objected to cartels it had previously "authorized" by nonobjection. Both cases involved section 3 rebate cartels, where the form of "authorization" was nonobjection and so there was no administrative act. The Court held that the restrictive rule of general administrative law does not apply to the cartel permission practice under the GWB, because the provisions of the GWB are specific departures from the general rule, which, under administrative law, withdraw it from the supplementing effect of the administrative procedure act. The Court held that cartel participants do, however, have a limited reliance interest which must be weighed against the public interest in implementation of the general cartel prohibition. The Court nevertheless held, since the GWB allows revocation of cartel permission with only future effect, only exceptional circumstances could justify a reliance interest, which would mandate continuing a permission beyond a short transition. The Court emphasized, because of the imperfect knowledge attending judgments of market behavior, the cartel authorities must be allowed flexibility, so that they can take time to observe effects on the market and can alter their legal decision accordingly.

> In this area, lack of reliable data concerning the interplay of competitive behavior of market participants causes extraordinary difficulties in investigation and evaluation of the facts material to decision . . . . Within the limits fixed by statute in the *Tatbestand*, the cartel authority is not precluded from reaching a different judgment of particular market activities as its observations and experiences suggest, nor is it restricted from requiring exempted cartels to undergo appropriate reviews, provided due regard is given to reliance interests.[252]

The problem confronted by the Court is a recurrent one in both American and German antitrust law. Flexible economic policy demands that enforcement authorities alter their policy with changed economic knowledge and conditions. Equity and Rule of Law security, however, demand recognizing justified reliance on prior policy. In German law, in some instances under intervention norms, the GWB deals with agency inactivity by limiting the time period of the authority to take action; if no action is taken within that time, the authority lapses and legal security is guaranteed (prohibition of a merger under section 22 II; forfeiture of excess profits under certain circumstances under section 37b I). In most instances, though, there is no provision for change from a policy of inaction to action. The German Federal Supreme Court has taken the position that it is not desirable to foreclose such changes, but has directed attention to implementing that change in an equitable way which balances the individual reliance interests with general welfare interests.[253] This balancing requires close attention to the time element and whether the change in policy affects only the future or the past as well.

6

Application of Antitrust Law

Chapters 4 and 5 considered differences in the substantive antitrust law of Germany and the United States. There it was shown that formulation of antitrust law, whether as judicial or administrative justice, and the form of its statement, whether in statute or judicial precedent, can affect Rule of Law security and the wisdom of policy decisions. However, the substantive law is not the only factor affecting antitrust policy decisions. Before a policy decision is reached, the substantive law and a factual situation must be brought together. This process presupposes a method of application of the law and a decision maker. Both can influence Rule of Law security and the wisdom of the policy decision. This chapter discusses the method of application of the law. Chapter 7 considers the decision makers.

According to German legal theory, application of the law entails subsuming a real life situation under a legal norm. In both the Federal Republic of Germany and the United States, lawyers incline to view this process as the application of the law to particular facts. However, the methods of this "application" differ so substantially between the two countries that it is only with great caution that both can be described as "application." This difference in the process of application contributes to understanding why antitrust is perceived in crisis in the United States but not in Germany.

Under German legal methods, the decision maker has primary responsibility for application of the law; under American methods that responsibility is held by the parties. Similarly, in German procedure the decision maker has primary control over the taking of evidence, while in

American procedure the parties do. Thus in American law, unlike in German law, decision making is separated from law application and fact investigation. In the ordinary case, when the issues remain simple, this separation of functions is tolerable. The substantive law may make a few such elements determinative. If the parties can readily identify these critical points, they can direct their legal arguments and factual investigations there. But as seen in Chapter 3, in antitrust law a policy decision is required because the law cannot preordain a single solution. The law cannot make one or two elements determinative. The policy decision requires a judgment of a complex factual situation in order to estimate a likely effect on general welfare. Because general welfare is indeterminate, the decision maker cannot possibly consider all relevant information; some selection must be made. In American antitrust law, that selection is not made by the decision maker, but by parties to litigation. As a result, the decision maker may be denied evidence he considers relevant, while he may be bombarded with evidence he considers irrelevant. Presentation of such evidence of course squanders time and other resources. In German cartel law, on the other hand, the decision maker by-and-large considers all the evidence he deems relevant and little he deems irrelevant.

ISSUE NARROWING: THE AMERICAN METHOD OF APPLICATION OF SUBSTANTIVE LAW

According to general German legal theory the judge applies a set of norms to a factual situation. A similar view occurs often in American law, but today is viewed skeptically, and has even been attacked as a "pretense." According to Edward Levi, "[t]he pretense is that the law is a system of known rules applied by a judge."[254] Levi's view is widely held in the United States and may even be the dominant view.[255] Consideration of the division of roles between judge and lawyer in the application of the law helps explain how this view could become dominant as well helps understand the American method of applying the law.

Roles of Participants in Issue Narrowing

The roles of the participants in the application of the law are extremely different between Germany and the United States. The roots of American civil procedure are found in an early form of procedure which arose to promote private settlement of subjective disputes and not to enforce an objective legal order. One who recalls these roots can more easily understand the very different roles in application of law. Indeed, it is here that the most critical differences between the American common law system and the German legal system are to be found.[256] This difference helps explain the different performances of German and American antitrust law.

In the United States the great majority of all cases are decided without the highly expensive common law trial. To say the cases are decided is not exactly correct. It is perhaps better to say: the conflicts are resolved. In cases that are settled without trial, the parties may call on the judge to determine particular issues, but it is up to the parties to conduct the "subsumption." There is no subsumption in the German sense. Whether the case goes to trial or not, principally the parties determine the issues which the judge or jury must decide. Although the forms of action have been abolished for over a century, the parties are still responsible for presenting their "theory of the case" to the court. The lawyers thus participate directly in the application of the law, and probably play the preeminent role in the usual case.[257] While it is no longer true, as it once was, that the court considers only the single narrow theory first raised in the complaint, it is still true that the court decides only the issues the parties present to it. Definition of those issues, though no longer plagued by the same formalism of the past, still plays a central role in American procedure. Moreover, the cost and clumsiness of common law trials, especially of adversary presentation, force limitation of the number of issues and their narrow definition to permit presentation to the judge (if legal issues) or to the fact finder, whether judge or jury (if factual issues). Today, unlike in earlier English procedure, the parties are not forced to choose one single issue, whether fact or law, to lay before the court.

The preeminent role of the parties in application of law carries over to factual investigation of the case. The parties independently inquire into what happened and prepare to present "their case" to the court. This procedure is quite expensive (in part because of redundancy, compared to procedure where the judge conducts one investigation under supervision of the parties) and leads to frequent settlements. Settlement is facilitated where the parties have clearly identified the issues and are able to predict with reasonable accuracy how the court would decide "the issue." For the lawyers to reach such a settlement, they need to know as exactly as possible how the court will decide. Wolfgang Fikentscher suggests that this need of the lawyers is an explanation for the complicated common law law of evidence, which should be considered along with the more usual explanation of jury control.[258] The point is well taken and might be made of the system of precedent as well. That would then explain the further observation that common law systems often permit predictions of final results more precise than European systems, which do not have binding precedents.[259]

The court decides those issues the parties cannot resolve themselves. The judge may determine purely legal issues before trial on motion of the parties upon conceded or assumed factual situations ("summary judgment"). The fact finder, who may be a judge or a jury, decides issues of fact and issues of mixed law and fact after taking of testimony at trial. The trial gives each party the opportunity to present his case to the fact finder. There the lawyer for the party calls "his" witnesses to testify favorably for his case. Having investigated the case beforehand, the lawyer is familiar with what his witnesses will say; ordinarily he will have prepared them. At trial, the lawyer asks them narrow questions designed to elicit only information favorable to his case. The opposing party then may interrogate the witnesses in order to develop facts favorable to his side or to impugn the witnesses' credibility. The fact finder remains passive. The judge may ask questions, but, even when acting as fact finder, is expected not to interfere in the lawyers' presentations.[260] The lawyers are to be vigorous advocates; they are to develop whatever facts they consider relevant. The fact finder is to choose between competing presentations as much as he is to find truth.[261] The judge oversees the process to see that the lawyer adheres to the rules of presentation.

In common law countries active participation of the parties' lawyers in resolution of the controversy and passivity of the decision maker are often thought to be important elements in the fulfillment of the guidance and the protection functions of the Rule of Law. Rules alone are not sufficient. Lon Fuller observed that it is common for those who emphasize the role of institutions over rules in the Rule of Law ("first courts, then rules") to argue that "[t]he essence of the rule of law consists in being assured your day in court."[262] Joseph Raz remarks, "[t]he litigants can be guided by law, only if the judge applies the law correctly."[263] When the parties' lawyers participate in application of the law, they are thought better able to guarantee that that application is correct. The parties would lose this protection if the judge were responsible for application of the law. Their control over application of the law also assures them that they cannot be told how to arrange their affairs any more than absolutely necessary to settle this controversy. When the parties are given their "day in court," they are protected against arbitrary action. According to Edward Levi, "[t]his is what makes the hearing fair, rather than any idea that the judge is completely impartial, for of course he cannot be completely so."[264] The passivity of the decision maker is thought to safeguard the fairness of the process and to avoid bias as much as possible. Because he does not investigate the case, he is not forced to develop tentative theories of the case to order his inquiry. The decision maker can, indeed he practically must, hold his judgment in suspension until both adversaries have completed their presentations.[265]

Policy Decisions and Issue Narrowing

Because of the leading role of the parties' lawyers in the investigation of the facts, in the application of the law, and in the presentation of witnesses, American procedure is designated in the United States an adversary system. Whatever may be the benefits and the drawbacks of an adversary system, it is reasonable to suspect that a system which relies on the pull of party self-interest to reach decisions will encounter greater strains when determining questions of policy than when deciding conflicting claims of right (or wrong). In an adversary system, the court decides only the issues presented to it. It considers only the evidence placed before it. Its ability to inquire beyond the evidence brought before it or to consider other legal questions is limited by its ability to prod the parties' lawyers into this activity. Since most cases are settled out of court, the overwhelming number of issues are decided without judicial consideration. That is ordinarily not troublesome, if they involve issues of private right rather than of public interest. The parties can be presumed to know their case best of all. If the parties are equally and well represented by counsel, the parties will know their rights as well as any court. Where, however, the issue to be decided is one of public policy rather than one of private right, even the fulfillment of this assumption cannot avoid serious strains on the adversary system.[266]

Another assumption of common law adversary litigation should be recognized: namely, that there is no substantial issue of public interest to be resolved in the dispute which is not adequately represented by the parties. Though this assumption may not be widely recognized, it seems undeniable. In the American system the parties largely control the litigation; their interest is to win their case, or at least to achieve the outcome most beneficial to them.[267] They are not interested in the public interest nor can they be expected to finance an inquiry into the general welfare. Issues they do not raise will not be considered. It should not be anticipated that the parties will raise issues of concern to the public interest but not to them. But the court cannot consider evidence not presented by the parties. If it must make a public interest decision in the litigation, likely as not, the court will make that decision without benefit of information relevant only to general welfare and not to the interests of the parties.[268]

Not only is it reasonable to anticipate that adversary application of law distorts policy judgments, it is also reasonable to suspect that policy judgments disrupt adversary presentation. While the parties know their own interests and are ordinarily able to explore and develop their cases based on those interests, there should not be the same expectations in cases based on public interest. Assuming that general welfare is something the parties can recognize, it is quite likely that one party may be better situated than the other to present its view of public interest to the court. Because public interest is nebulous and indeterminate, it provides less of a bound to adversary presentation than does a question of private right. There is only so much that can be said about one individual's right, but this is not so of general welfare interests. The policy question thus increases possibilities for abuse of liberties (for example, discovery) granted by adversary presentation. To what extent can public policy questions fit within adversary litigation? The present crisis in antitrust is a frustrating example of the problem.

Issue Narrowing in American Antitrust Law

The "legal" question in American antitrust law is often no more definite than whether a challenged restraint or merger permits an adequate level of competition. "The true test of legality is whether the restraint imposed is such as merely regulates and perhaps thereby promotes competition or whether it is such as may suppress or even destroy competition."[269] Beyond this rule lies not law, but "antitrust analysis." The rule of reason does not supply rules,[270] but mandates an "inquiry." The mode of "antitrust analysis" has a tentative nature, for it is merely the implementation of the grater rule of effect on competition. It has two complementary categories: plainly anticompetitive agreements are per se unlawful; other agreements are subject to an all encompassing inquiry to determine lawfulness. "In either event, the purpose of the analysis is to form a judgment about the competitive significance of the restraint."[271] While certain restraints have been classified per se unlawful because experience has shown them almost always to affect competition negatively, such "broad generalization[s] about the social utility of particular commercial practices" are subject to reconsideration and recall should later experience show otherwise. Here is the flexibility in the law, for the only rule is the rule of competition. Were all antitrust law per se rules, there would be an "unintended and undesirable rigidity in the law."[272]

An investigation into how issue narrowing has affected antitrust policy decisions is beyond the scope of this work, but not consideration of the speculative question: Can such an "antitrust analysis" fit into common law adversary litigation? The needs of common law adjudication push resolutely toward issue narrowing. With narrowed issues, the parties' lawyers can negotiate. With narrowed issues, they can prepare their cases to present to the court. But how are issues narrowed? Parties are eliminated, or their interests are combined. Questions of fact or of law are conceded or eliminated. The lawyers make an issue, or a handful, determinative of the outcome of the case.

Effect on competition is no narrow issue. The parties' lawyers could not apply a rule of competition themselves, nor could they prepare to present a case based on competition alone. Thus the courts resort to "antitrust analysis." But adversary litigation continues to have its effect. It demands that "antitrust analysis" be narrowed to clearly identified particular issues. It pushes to make one issue determinative, whether factual or legal, toward a particular formulation of analysis, namely:

if A, then R.

Adversary litigation presses to reject competing forms of analysis. While a multipath analysis such as

if A + B
or B + C
or C + A
then R,

might still be possible in simple cases, which the system could treat as three separate rules, it must reject such an analysis as unmanageable when the case becomes more complex or when the number of possible combinations increases. Similarly, adversary litigation presses resolutely to reject variable factor analyses such as:

$$\text{if } (aA + bB + cC)\ D \text{ then } R.$$

The adversary system must tend to reject both multipath and variable factor analyses, because they pose difficult dilemmas for the lawyers. Each factor's importance depends on the other's. Many routings to the goal are possible. Without knowing how a particular factor will be weighted, the lawyers cannot surrender any, nor can they know on which to place the emphasis of their preparation. They do not know which factor or which path the decision maker will deem the most important.

The common law system of dispute resolution pushes to eliminate the competing paths, to cut out necessary weighting, and to force multipath and variable factor analyses into a single path analysis, with preferably a single issue question. Practically the lawyers cannot independently investigate and put before the court too many issues. The 13 years the IBM case spent in first instance before the government finally dropped it is vivid evidence how long an antitrust case can take.

This problem has been recognized. The solution usually suggested is introduction of hard-hearted judges who will force the lawyers to narrow issues. But that may only make one issue determinative to the exclusion of other considerations. Vertical merger cases exemplify the resultant tensions. Some courts make foreclosure the issue; others resist simplifying the question of competition, but then confront difficult problems of litigation and settlement.[273]

While for this work the effect of issue narrowing and adversary presentation on antitrust policy decisions must remain speculative, the effects of antitrust policy decisions on adversary litigation are already documented. Sometimes dubbed simply "the big case," the complex antitrust case has been the subject of substantial research since 1950. The big antitrust case usually, if not always, requires what has been termed here a policy decision.[274] Already in 1951 a distinguished committee of the Judicial Conference of the United States (the Prettyman Report) studied the "acute major problem" of the big antitrust case, and reported that the unnecessary consumption of resources and resulting "confusion" and "uncertainty" were of such magnitude that, if permitted to continue, they "might threaten the judicial process itself in respect to complex controversies."[275] Official and unofficial consideration of the big case has continued regularly ever since with no satisfactory solution yet in sight. Something of a culmination, at least for antitrust cases, was reached in 1978 when President Carter appointed a presidential commission (The National Commission for Review of Antitrust Laws and Procedures) to inquire into the unreasonable protraction of these cases which seem to "drag out indefinitely."[276]

Reports prepared at the Commission's request expressed serious reservations about the wisdom of continued use of traditional methods in antitrust cases. The Special Advisory Panel on Ethical Issues in Complex Antitrust Litigation urged that "faced with overwhelming evidence that the present system in antitrust and other complex cases generally does not provide effective and speedy justice," the commission should call upon the American Bar Association to consider whether such litigation should not be tried on the basis of "ethical premises very different from those that presently exist."[277] The Report of the Empirical Case Studies Project added "the failure of the judicial system . . . raises concerns about the viability of using the courts as the major architect of antitrust policy.[278]

The Commission itself did not view so gloomy the prospects of adapting adversary litigation to decision of complex antitrust cases. The Commission found, in accord with commentary and the Empirical Case Studies Project, that the greatest amount of time in complex antitrust litigation is consumed in pretrial phases of independent investigation (discovery) by the parties' lawyers. It found excessive proliferation of claims and defenses and abusive discovery requests. The Commission recommended the use of time limits and sanctions to control and limit party investigation. Through such measures it hoped to set a two year limit for pretrial phase investigation (counting from when the case is formally filed). The Commission emphasized in its very first recommendation that "[i]n complex or potentially protracted cases, judicial management should begin early and be applied continuously and actively, based on knowledge of the circumstances of each case."[279] The judge should control pretrial investigation and help narrow issues.[280] The Commission called for increased use of judicial notice and of stipulations of the parties, though, it noted, of course not for questions "involving motive, intent, or reasonableness."[281] The Commission recognized that problems of delay in antitrust cases might lie "in the adversary system" itself and conceded that its recommendation, for active judges managing cases with which they are familiar, runs counter to traditional American notions of the role of the trial judge.[282] The Commission asked district courts to consider the possibility of assigning judges to antitrust cases who are inclined "to the exercise of firm and efficient case management" to try complex antitrust cases.[283] The Commission rejected as unwise, however, a proposal which would have institutionalized such judges in a "special roster"; that is, antitrust cases would have automatically been referred to judges specifically designated to hear such cases.[284] The Commission therefore rejected the one substantial institutional change in procedure it considered.

Critical Observations on the Suitability of Issue Narrowing in Antitrust Law

The policy decision which can be expected from issue narrowing in complex antitrust cases is likely to be poor. The judge is asked to decide what is the right level of competition in the community. The parties agree or, under the compulsion of the judge acting without investigation, are forced to agree to make a few issues determinative. Without investigation, what can guide this issue narrowing – the parties' self-interest? The judge's own preconceptions of general welfare? Judicial practice in prior cases of uncertain similarity? It is certainly fair to question how well such litigation about the "issue" reflects general welfare. Competing and conflicting interests may have been combined; important issues compressed, or eliminated – all without investigation. No justification relating the issue narrowing to the facts is made. One issue may be made determinative of the proper effect on competition. Advocates of a rule of reason inquiry should ask themselves: Isn't this what we wanted to avoid by not applying a casuistic code of specific forbidden practices? When one economic factor is made determinative, won't anticompetitive practices slip through and procompetitive practices get caught in the net? Doesn't the effect on competition depend on the context?

The judge can hardly be expected to know of effect on competition and general welfare in such a case. He is thrown back on the evidence the parties present. While trial judges can prod the parties to investigate, appellate judges rarely have even this opportunity. But the opportunities open to trial judges should not be overestimated. A trial judge need not ask more than a few questions or call more than one witness, before being accused of "taking over" the parties' case. He is told to keep his "mouth shut."[285] But the silent judge is forced to make policy decisions based on imperfect information.[286] Where does he turn? To his own experience? Possible, but usually not considered acceptable. To precedents? Authoritative, but often not relevant. He cannot investigate.

For 30 years proposals to expedite American antitrust litigation have made the same recommendation: The judge must be strong; he must force the parties to early issue narrowing and encourage them to agree as much as possible on factual statements and legal contentions; he must control and limit the lawyers' investigation and development of the case. What does this mean for policy decisions? Either the judge takes over the case to get the information he needs for his decision, or he makes his decision with less than a complete picture of the actual situation. Common law tradition lets the lawyers control the litigation. But if the judge is to make informed general welfare decisions, he cannot leave it to the lawyers to narrow the issues if they don't well represent public interest. Yet there is danger in allowing the judge to narrow issues on incomplete information. Per se rules are a form of narrowing the issues; issue narrowing may not ever work well where per se rules do not work.

Yet, without narrowed issues, the outlook for adversary litigation absorbing complex antitrust cases hardly appears favorable, as can be recognized after reflection on some history – the history of the trial of complex antitrust cases and the history of common law procedure. Ever since there have been complex antitrust cases requiring important policy decisions, there have been mammoth and long adversary battles, whether in trial, pretrial, or on appeal. Since 1950 these cases have been of sufficient frequency to lead to intense study and reform attempts. Success has not been substantial. Now recall the history of common law procedure. Adversary presentation and issue narrowing developed alongside the forms of action.[287] The forms of action set limits to the trial. While the lawyers were allowed to control the case, they could do so only within rigid confines. The forms of action were abolished a century ago. The antitrust laws, however, set no comparable limits. From the Prettyman Report to the Report of the National Commission for Review of Antitrust Laws and Procedures the role recommended for the trial judge in complex antitrust cases is that of manager. The trial judge is to provide the control the statute does not. Yet that role is contrary to common law traditions.[288] If American antitrust litigation is to be made to work, Americans need to recognize that a significant break with tradition is required. Those seeking reform should take steps to assure that this break can be made.

SUBSUMPTION: THE GERMAN METHOD OF APPLICATION OF SUBSTANTIVE LAW

The application of the GWB has posed difficult problems for traditional German legal methods. Nevertheless, the basic German method of norm and subsumption has allowed the Germans to avoid some of the most troublesome problems chronically experienced in application of American antitrust law. German methods do not force antitrust policy decisions to become decisions of narrow issues. On the contrary, German methods require decision makers to consider every element of the *Tatbestand*, or "all the issues," so to speak. Where policy decisions are required, German decision makers are outfitted with means to judge general welfare. They are not bound by the presentations of "parties": They may hear anyone affected by their decision, even those who could not be "parties" in a civil conflict. Where application of the GWB has posed problems for German methods has been in giving form to the norm.

Roles of Participants in Subsumption

German legal methods have no issue narrowing in the American sense. A given legal consequence can be applied if and only if a given factual situation satisfies each and every element of the *Tatbestand* of the relevant norm. Subsumption of the factual situation under the norm therefore requires consideration of every *Tatbestand* element in every case. German university legal education turns on teaching the legal essentials of subsumption: the choice of the norm and the identification of the relevant *Tatbestand* elements and legal consequences.

The judge or other decision maker is fully responsible for the application of the law. Although the parties often have rights to express their views of the law and may have indirect control over the law applied through their control over the facts, the maxim *da mihi factum, dabo tibi ius* (give me the facts, I will give you the law) applies fully.[289] The judge is not bound by the legal contentions of the parties; he may rest his decision on a norm other than that suggested by them. The parties cannot avoid application of a legal norm by submitting only part of their dispute; for example, they could not avoid a norm invalidating a contract, even though the party protected by the norm is willing to accept the contract as valid.[290] Before the judge takes evidence, in every case he must proof the allegations of the plaintiff to see that the alleged factual situation fulfills the norm the specific allegations fulfill the *Tatbestand,* and the individual observations fulfill the particular element of the *Tatbestand* (*Schlüßigkeitsprüfung*).[291] The defendant's response, if any, to the allegations of the plaintiff is without significance for this proofing. Here, the judge begins subsumption, albeit tentatively.

For subsumption, the judge or other decision maker must select the norm and proof whether the factual situation fulfills the elements of the *Tatbestand* of the norm. The judge or other decision maker works from both ends – from determining the factual situation and from choosing and construing the appropriate legal norm – until he reaches a subsumption susceptible norm and can subsume the facts of the case under the elements of its *Tatbestand.* Necessarily he must direct his attention from facts to law and back to facts again. For he can determine what facts are relevant only in respect to at least his tentative choice of norm, and ordinarily he can understand the particular elements of the *Tatbestand* of the norm only in relation to the facts.[292] But there is no issue narrowing. While the judge must make a tentative choice of norm or norms, he need not limit the inquiry up until he determines that the factual situation fulfills all the elements of the *Tatbestand* of one particular norm. At that point, all that remains is for the decision maker to draw the consequences imposed by objective law and order the particular legal consequence which follows fulfillment of the particular norm.

The German judge or other decision maker does not have the same monopolistic role in the development of the factual investigation of the case, which he has in the application of the law. Here the decision maker shares control with the parties or other participants, to an extent which varies for different types of procedures and tasks. German legal science uses two pairs of contrasting principles of procedure to describe how the decision maker must share control: party disposition/official control principles (*Dispositions-/Offizialmaximen*) and party presentation/judicial investigation principles (*Verhandlungs-/Untersuchungsmaximen*). One factor that contributes to determine which half of each pair applies is the extent to which the procedure concerned considers questions of private or public interest.[293] For example, the party disposition and party presentation principles ordinarily prevail in civil procedure. The party disposition principle means the parties control the initiation of the suit and its subject matter (*Streitgegenstand*); they are free to withdraw the suit from the decision maker whenever they wish. The party presentation principle means the parties control the production of the evidence necessary for the decision. What they do not produce, the decision maker will not consider. This infringement on the court's duty to find the truth is considered acceptable because civil procedure is concerned more with reaching a relative truth between the parties than with finding objective truth. Nevertheless, even when the party presentation principle applies, the duty of elucidation (*Aufklärungspflicht*) pursuant to Code of Civil Procedure ("ZPO") § 139, requires the judge to ask questions to insure that the parties fully explain the legally significant facts of their submissions.[294] Where the official control and judicial investigation principles prevail, the decision maker himself is responsible for invocation of the proceeding and for production of the evidence necessary for decision. The official control principle applies rarely in judicial procedure, but is common in administrative procedure. In criminal procedure a kind of highly modified form of official control principle applies. State authorities are responsible for initiating proceedings, but that responsibility is split between two independent authorities: The court can be active only after the prosecutor brings an accusation which the court determines is adequate to warrant an investigation (*Anklageprinzip* – principle of prosecution). The principle of judicial investigation applies in a few areas of civil procedure, but applies generally throughout criminal and administrative procedure. Where it prevails, the decision maker must uncover the facts necessary for application of the norm and there is no burden of proof on the parties or participants. Where the party presentation and party disposition principles or the principle of prosecution apply, the decision maker's duty of investigation under the principle of judicial investigation is limited by the facts which form the basis of the plaintiff's complaint or the prosecutor's accusation. In areas of particular public interest – often where both official control and judicial investigation principles prevail – the procedure does not recognize "parties," but only "participants." Here, the decision maker's responsibility to discover objective truth is much greater than in cases where findings of relative truth to settle conflicts between parties are sufficient.

In all forms of German procedure the actual proof taking is nonadversarial and largely in the hands of the decision maker. Essentially the judge or other decision maker conducts a hearing of witnesses under the supervision of the parties or participants. The degree and form of this supervision varies with the type of procedure.[295] In judicial procedures the judge calls witnesses for the court and the parties both. The parties do not present their own witnesses and their preparation of witnesses is held to be unethical. There is no presentation of separate cases for each side.

The judge is responsible for questioning witnesses. The parties ask supplemental questions to fill out the witness's testimony. For the judge to be able to question witnesses intelligently, he must necessarily have knowledge of the case beforehand.[296]

The common law lawyer, accustomed to adversary presentation and a central role for the lawyer in the application of the law, is likely to be suspicious of the dominant role of the German judge in application of law. Where is the guarantee the judge applies the law correctly? What assurance is there that the defendant gets his day in court? German law includes many mechanisms to assure correct application of the law. Perhaps most important is the requirement that every major decision (and many minor ones) must have a statement of reasons (*Begründung*) and is subject to appeal. In the university, German jurists learn to work with norms to permit subsumption. In the mandatory multiple year practical internship which follows the university education, they learn, above all, how to write a judgment, which incorporates the statement of reasons. The German judgment is a highly formalized statement that includes the legal outcome of the case (*Tenor*), the factual findings (*Tatbestand*), and the legal assessment of the factual situation (*Entscheidungsgründe*). The judgment explains to the parties the reasons for the decision and furnishes the appellate courts with a basis for review of trial court action. Appeal in Germany is generally available for factual as well as legal questions. The first level appellate court may take additional evidence to fill out or correct lower court judgments. Besides these important protections, German law also guarantees to the parties the right to express their position on all material facts, and, in court proceedings, their position on questions of law. In criminal and administrative procedures participants have the right (through their lawyer) to review the official dossier compiled by the prosecutor or administrative authority.[297] In most forms of procedure, oral hearings open to the public are required. Moreover, German decision makers are usually professionally trained as such and are subject to bureaucratic control when they inadequately fulfill the duties of their office.[298]

Subsumption in German Cartel Law

The German requirement that the decision maker must always proof every element of the *Tatbestand* before he can order the corresponding legal consequence precludes issue narrowing in the American sense. The advantage of this method for antitrust policy decisions is that investigation and legal interpretation each proceed apace, accompanying one another, without the decision maker having to make a final decision until the eventual subsumption. Of course, he must make intermediate decisions about what evidence to take, but he can alter these as necessary. He can investigate different theories of liability and can consider different measures of competition simultaneously. He need not reject the multipath and the variable factor analyses. If he must simplify the basis for his decision (say on an aspect of competition), it is either because he has insufficient factual information or because of limitations of economic inquiry. It is not because he is compelled to simplification by the method of decision making. While the law can do little to overcome deficiencies of economic analysis, the GWB tries to assure that the decision maker has the necessary factual basis for his decision.

Cartel law decisions are made subject to three different kinds of procedure: civil, criminal, and administrative. As was shown in Chapter 5, prohibition norms are enforced in all three kinds of procedure, however only future-oriented legal consequences can be ordered when administrative procedure is invoked. Permission norms and intervention norms, on the other hand, are applied only in administrative procedure. In civil procedure the decision maker is an ordinary court. In enforcement of the cartel law, the party disposition and party presentation principles prevail; the court considers only the factual conflict specified by the parties and the evidence they produce. In regulatory infraction proceedings the decision is split between cartel authorities, the court, and, in a sense, the affected party. The cartel authorities have the position and authority of a prosecutor and are subject to the limitations imposed on prosecutors by the criminal code. If the party affected is unwilling to accept the cartel authority's order to pay a quasi-criminal penalty, trial follows subject to the prosecution and judicial investigation principles. The court investigates the factual incident subject to the framework imposed by the earlier finding of the administrative authority. In administrative procedure the decision maker is the cartel authority. The official control and judicial investigation principles prevail. The cartel authority initiates the investigation itself (within the limits of its authority) or upon application of some concerned person (§ 51 I GWB). The cartel authority is responsible for locating the evidence required for application of the norm. To enable the authorities to carry out this role, the statute gives them, subject to controls, wide-ranging investigative powers (§§ 46, 54, 55).[299] Moreover, the cartel authorities may hear a wider range of persons than is usual in judicial procedure. Administrative procedure knows no parties, only participants; participants include not only cartels and enterprises subject to the potential decision, but also the person who applied for the investigation, and such other persons who have applied and have been acknowledged by the cartel authorities to be participants because their interests are materially affected by the potential decision (§51 II 4).[300]

How does this stepped system of procedures affect antitrust policy decisions? Policy judgments are concentrated in intervention and permission norms. These norms are applied only in administrative procedure. The principle of judicial investigation applies. The decision maker is not limited by the submissions of parties, but is obligated to investigate the material facts himself. He must find the factual basis to justify his decision. Participation in that investigation need not be limited to opposing parties, but can extend to a wider range of participants. So far as a policy judgment occasionally may be required to enforce a prohibition norm, administrative procedure is available, but only to direct future-oriented legal consequences. Thus the legal system works to assist, rather than to hinder, investigation of general welfare.

It has not been without difficulty that the German legal system has accommodated antitrust policy decisions. Subsumption is facilitated by clear and precise concepts; it is complicated by indefinite legal concepts. Yet it is the latter which are almost always used as central elements of the *Tatbestände* of antitrust policy norms. Eberhard Günther, himself one of the drafters of the GWB, explained: "[t]he use of indefinite legal concepts, namely . . . of competition-based elements of the *Tatbestand*, is explainable by the fact that complex economic relations are not suited for integration into a set catalog of legal concepts."[301] The less sharp the concept is, the more complex the material *Tatbestand* element, the more thoroughly the decision maker must examine the factual situation. Gerd Pfeiffer, president of the cartel senate of the German Federal Supreme Court, observed that the use of indefinite legal concepts in the GWB "burdens the fact finder up to the limits of the carrying out of his duty."[302] The tensions created are particularly evident in the relation between the decision maker and the reviewing courts. Who should decide what? Decisions of the cartel authorities are subject to an unusually comprehensive review, much more like that accorded a trial court decision than the proofing normally given administrative decisions. Günther has argued:

> A legislature that uses value filled, general-clause-like indefinite concepts as standards for decision, forces the party charged with applying the law to

> engage in policy making and forces that party to take over setting normative standards. It is hard to call such *filling out* of the legal concepts "statutory interpretation"; what are really involved are policy decisions forming and developing the economic system.[303]

Günther is led to question the "nearly unlimited authority for review" of the decisions of the cartel authorities by the appeals courts:

> If the cartel authority as an administrative agency is given the policy function of establishing normative standards, then the appellate court may not routinely function in place of the agency setting the norm; the appellate court should not substitute its conceptions for the cartel authority's policies in filling out indefinite legal concepts. Rather, political decisions of the administration should be reviewed only for their conformity with the limits set by applicable law; otherwise these decisions are subject to the properly exercised *pflichtgemässen* discretion of the competent agency. A political decision is characterized by the fact that it could have come out another way without violating applicable law.[304]

With these remarks, Gunther seems to align himself with those who argue that the indefinite legal concepts give the administration room for judgment (*Beurteilungsspielraum*).[305]

While the difficulties with subsumption of real life cases under indefinite legal concepts may have contributed to the frequent amendments to the GWB (three within the last decade), they have not given rise to the same perception of crisis found in the United States. Difficulties in subsumption have not caused Rule of Law problems comparable to those in the United States. Perhaps this is also because of certain institutional arrangements. As already shown, the GWB has a restraining function by largely limiting the effects of policy decisions to the future. The control of the decision maker over production of evidence considered in this section also works to prevent the interminable law suits experienced in the United States. Moreover, those charged with applying the law, particularly those charged with policy decisions, are experienced with the law and frequently know the affected industries. The political tensions that do exist between first instance and review, caused by the indefinite legal concepts, are largely centralized in one highly visible chain of three decision makers: the Federal Cartel Authority in West Berlin, the cartel senate of the Court of Appeals for West Berlin (*Kammergericht*), and the cartel senate of the Federal Supreme Court. The following chapter considers characteristics of these three organizations.

7

Antitrust Policy Decision Makers

No system of law can be divorced from the people charged with implementing it. Who the decision makers are and how they relate one to another necessarily affect how the law is realized. When decision makers are less bound by legal rules, personnel and organizational factors assume greater importance in predicting their decisions than when rules spell out the legal result more clearly. What can be expected of decision makers may become even more important for prediction of legal decisions than what can be expected of the legal rules themselves.[306] Thus the personnel making decisions may influence the protection and guidance interests of the Rule of Law and the wisdom of policy decisions as much as the legal rules. Where specific rules are avoided to allow decision makers a certain freedom, such as in antitrust, personnel and organization are crucial.

The decision makers of German cartel law are largely centralized, coordinated, and collegiate. They are usually specialized and professionalized. In short, they are bureaucratic. The decision makers of American antitrust law, in contrast, are largely not centralized, not coordinated, and not collegiate. They are less specialized and less professionalized than their German counterparts. They are not bureaucratic. The German approach was adopted to produce the usual benefits claimed for bureaucracy – precision, definiteness, continuity, and speed.[307] The characteristics of the German approach to cartel law are not untypical for German law generally, though they are more pronounced in cartel law than elsewhere and, within cartel law itself, they are more pronounced for policy decisions than for other decisions. The

American approach basically just carries over to antitrust law the usual American approach to litigation. It is used to preserve neutrality, open-mindedness, and independence of the decision maker – in short, his autonomy. It seeks to avoid what has been said to be the principal vice of bureaucracy: the tendency "to judge too swiftly in terms of the familiar that which is not yet fully known."[308]

The structures of decision making in German and American antitrust law are strikingly different. Differences generally typical of the gulf between the German and American judicial systems are further accented by the sometime use of administrative procedure in the Federal Republic of Germany. When legal rules do not determine the decision, the extra-legal justification provided by each system for the decision is quite different.

American antitrust law prefers the autonomous, fresh decision maker. Where legal rules cannot determine the solution, the fact finder's neutrality and the guarantee that those presenting the case fully argue their positions justifies the decision. The fact finder's neutrality is protected by its autonomy of decision. So long as it hears all the evidence, unless its judgment is clearly erroneous or could be reached by no reasonable fact finder, it is accepted. The fact finder need not provide a particular justification for its determination. Its freshness protects its neutrality; it is not required to place a factual situation in some abstract order.

German cartel law, on the other hand, prefers the responsible, expert decision maker. Where legal rules cannot determine the solution, the fact finder's scientific argumentation and the guarantee that argumentation can be fully proofed justifies the decision. The fact finder's responsibility is promoted by its clear identification through centralization, collegiality, and publicity. Its factual findings must be carefully reasoned and are subject to review, to further testing through additional evidence, and to refinement. Professionalization and organization assure an expert and experienced fact finder.

DECISION MAKERS IN GERMAN CARTEL LAW

A variety of decision makers have responsibilities under the German cartel law. The administrative decision makers include the Federal Cartel Authority (*Bundeskartellamt* – BKartA), the provincial cartel authorities, and the federal minister for economics. The administrative authorities apply permission and intervention norms, act as prosecutors in quasi-criminal enforcement of prohibition norms, and can prohibit conduct in violation of prohibition norms. Judicial decision makers are civil panels of the ordinary courts. District courts handle private enforcement of prohibition norms and are authorized in such cases to order discontinuance of prohibited conduct and to award damages for injuries sustained. The courts of appeals review decisions of the cartel authorities and of the district courts for errors in fact and law, and act as courts of first instance in GWB quasi-criminal prosecutions. The Federal Supreme Court reviews decisions of the courts of appeals for errors in law. Yet another decision maker is the Monopolies Commission, which is an independent committee, and which has certain advisory duties. Despite this mosaic of decision makers, antitrust policy decisions are concentrated in one chain: the Federal Cartel Authority in West Berlin as first instance, the court of appeals for West Berlin (known as the *Kammergericht*) as second instance for questions of fact and law, and the Supreme Court as final instance for questions of law only.

The Federal Cartel Authority

The Key Role of the Federal Cartel Authority in Policy Decisions

The Federal Cartel Authority plays a preeminent role in enforcement of German cartel law. Policy decisions, insofar as they are not given to the federal minister for economics for an overt political decision, are largely centralized with the Federal Cartel Authority. In other areas of cartel law, the Federal Cartel Authority has a leadership role. Although it has no control over decisions of the provincial cartel authorities or of the regular courts, it has important powers to coordinate the activities of these bodies in enforcement of the GWB.

In Chapter 5 it was shown that policy decisions under the GWB are concentrated in application of permission and intervention norms. The application of permission norms is almost completely centralized with the Federal Cartel Authority. The Federal Cartel Authority has exclusive competence for some permission norms (§§ 4, 6, 7); for the others (§§ 2, 3, 5, 5a, 5b, 20, 21) it has de facto controlling competence, since § 44 I No. 1d of the GWB gives the Federal Cartel Authority exclusive competence whenever the economic effect extends over more than one province.[309] In case of mergers, the possibility of ministerial permission arises only after the Federal Cartel Authority exercises its authority to prohibit the merger (under § 24). Application of the intervention norms is only somewhat less centralized with the Federal Cartel Authority. The Federal Cartel Authority has exclusive competence for some interventions (mergers § 24, resale price maintenance, so far as it is still allowed the book trade §§ 16, 17, and resale price recommendations § 38a), and preeminent control of the other intervention norms by virtue of the rule of § 44 I No. 1d. The provincial cartel authorities do play a more significant role in application of the abuse control over market-dominating enterprises; they also have a consultative role for mergers affecting enterprises located within their respective provinces. By and large, the provincial authorities concentrate on application of prohibition norms (§§ 1, 15, 25, 26) and of the abuse control (§ 22).[310] As already shown, however, application of prohibition norms requires fewer policy judgments than application of other GWB norms. Insofar as the provincial cartel authorities do have competence, however, their competence is exclusive. As is usual in German federalism, the provincial authorities are independent of federal authorities even when enforcing federal law.[311] The Federal Cartel Authority has no direct control over decisions of the provincial authorities; the GWB does, however, give the Federal Cartel Authority a coordinating role and a position of persuasion in application of the law by both the provincial authorities and the district courts.

The GWB gives the Federal Cartel Authority the status of participant in all administrative proceedings of provincial cartel authorities under § 51 III. It has the same rights as any participant. In particular, it may contest the jurisdiction of the provincial authority and may take interlocutory appeals from adverse jurisdictional holdings (§ 52 I). It may express its position regarding the investigation and must on application be called for an oral hearing (§ 53 I). It may inspect the dossier of the provincial authority "so far as knowledge thereof is necessary for exercise or defense of [its] legal interests" (§ 29 VwVfG). Perhaps most important, it may appeal decisions of the provincial authorities (§ 62 II). The provincial authorities have no comparable participation rights in proceedings of the Federal Cartel Authority. The GWB requires that the various authorities notify each other whenever they begin administrative or quasi-criminal investigations against enterprises or other nonnatural individuals (§ 45 I-II), and to turn investigations over to the other, whenever the other's competence is indicated (§ 45 III).

The GWB gives the Federal Cartel Authority a similar role in private cases. In every civil case in which a controversy depends on the GWB or is based on a cartel agreement, the GWB requires the court to notify the Federal Cartel Authority. Upon request, the court must furnish the Federal Cartel Authority with copies of all pleadings, protocols of testimony taken, and decisions (§ 90 I). In practice, the court usually requires the parties to file extra copies of all documents for the Federal Cartel Authority.[312] Unlike in provincial administrative proceedings, the GWB does not give the Federal Cartel Authority the status of a party in the case, so it cannot appeal the final decision. It nevertheless has wide-ranging rights of participation whenever the president of the Federal Cartel Authority determines that participation is "appropriate" for "protection of the public interest" (§ 90 II). Practically, the president's decision is largely incontestable.[313] If the president decides to exercise these rights, the Federal Cartel Authority may make written declarations, may present evidence, and may dispatch a representative authorized to ask questions of the parties and witnesses at the trial (§ 90 II). Critics have voiced concerns that Federal Cartel Authority participation may work one-sidedly to disadvantage the parties subject to the GWB norm, particularly when the Federal Cartel Authority itself is simultaneously investigating the concerned party.[314] When the economic effect of the controversy is limited to one province, the appropriate provincial cartel authority substitutes for the Federal Cartel Authority in the trial court in all respects except the original notification (§ 90 III).

Organization of the Federal Cartel Authority

The Federal Cartel Authority is an independent higher federal agency (*Bundesoberbehörde*) assigned to the competence of the federal minister for economics (§ 48).[315] As a higher federal agency, the Federal Cartel Authority is competent for the entire country. Its independent status precludes the minister from withdrawing questions from it. Because the minister has parliamentary responsibility for the Federal Cartel Authority, he may issue it directives for exercise of its duties. Whether the Federal Cartel Authority itself is supposed to exercise a mandate for competition policy is disputed. In support of the position that it is, is raised the statutory requirement that the Federal Cartel Authority report to parliament periodically, not only on its own activities, but "as well as concerning the situation and development in its area of competence" (§ 50 I 1).[316]

The Federal Cartel Authority is not hierarchically organized. It is vertically deconcentrated. It consists of a president, several staff sections, and nine decision sections (*Beschlußabteilungen*). The decision sections reach the decisions assigned the Federal Cartel Authority under the GWB (§ 48 II 1); the president has largely administrative duties. The nonhierarchical form of organization was adopted to give the decision sections a degree of independence comparable to that enjoyed by courts.[317] The decision sections are organized generally along industry lines. Specific decision sections, however, are responsible for certain tasks without regard to industry; these tasks are drawn from the permission and prohibition norms. Though the president has no direct control over decisions of the decision sections, he determines this organization. He prepares an order of business (*Geschäftsordnung*), which abstractly assigns matters coming before the Federal Cartel Authority to the various panels. The order of business requires approval of the minister. The president may withdraw a matter from one decision section and give it to another only if the order of business incorporates a reservation for such a matter or is amended.[318]

Decision sections decide in panels of three, made up of a chairman and two assessors (*Beisitzende*). The nine decision sections presently consist of about six or seven members each; the chairman of the individual decision section determines which assessors participate in a particular case.[319] The chairman may not, however, direct assessors how to vote; the decision is collegiate.[320] Assessors must be qualified for judicial or high administrative office, and the chairman, as a rule, for judicial office (§ 48 IV 2). The former requirement permits economists to be assessors, although the latter can only exceptionally be chairmen. The Federal Cartel Authority has made liberal use of this provision; typically a third to a half of assessors are economists.[321] Service with the Federal Cartel Authority is ordinarily a life-long career. While there is the possibility for political input in the initial appointment,[322] members of the decision sections enjoy life tenure (§ 48 IV 1) and thus can be dismissed only under very limited circumstances. In its 28-year existence, the Federal Cartel Authority has had only two presidents; the first retired at age 65 in 1976.

The provincial cartel authorities do not share the independence enjoyed by the decision sections of the Federal Cartel Authority. They are integral parts of hierarchically organized provincial ministries of economics.

The Relationship Between the Federal Ministry for Economics and the Federal Cartel Authority

While the Federal Cartel Authority is an independent higher federal agency it falls within the competence of the federal minister for economics. The minister has parliamentary responsibility for the Federal Cartel Authority. While he cannot withdraw questions from it, he may issue specific and general directives to the Federal Cartel Authority for the exercise of its duties.[323] While the propriety of the issuance of case specific directives has been questioned, it is generally acknowledged to be within the minister's authority.[324] In the GWB's 28-year history, only once has a minister made use of this authority.[325] Under general principles of administrative law, the minister may not direct the Federal Cartel Authority to act contrary to statute or to duty.[326] Practically, this means he can only direct the Federal Cartel Authority to act within the limits of its discretion. In any case, the minister would have difficulty making case specific directives effective. The decision sections decide secretly in panels of three; a member subject to a directive could always claim to have been outvoted by his colleagues.

The minister has made greater, though still not frequent use of his authority to issue general directives to the Federal Cartel Authority. Five times – all since 1971 – a minister has issued such directives.[327] The minister's general directives are regarded in commentary as of two forms: directions for uniform interpretation of indefinite legal concepts in the law (*Auslegungsrichtlinien*) and directions for uniform application of the law (*Anwendungsrichtlinien*). The latter, which essentially direct the Federal Cartel Authority in the exercise of its discretion, are thought more likely to create the danger of a directive to act contrary to statute or duty. Such a general directive would be just as invalid as a comparable case-specific directive.[328] The GWB requires publication of all general directives in the *Bundesanzeiger* (Federal Register) (§ 49). The minister can bind only the Federal Cartel Authority with his directives; he cannot bind the provincial authorities or the courts.[329]

The minister has other formal and informal ways to influence the Federal Cartel Authority. He is responsible for initial appointments to the decision sections (§ 48 II). He must comment on the Federal Cartel Authority's biennial report (§ 50 II). He resolves certain conflicts between the Federal Cartel Authority and other governmental authorities responsible for regulated industries (§§ 44 II, 102 II). From time to time, the minister has published statements of how the Federal Ministry for Economics interprets the GWB, such as in a set of guidelines known as the *Kooperationsfibel*, which affect interpretation of the law, though they are not general directives.[330] Moreover, informal and regular cooperation between the Federal Cartel Authority and the Ministry is said to be the rule; the president of the Federal Cartel Authority regularly participates in the meetings of the section chiefs of the Ministry in Bonn.[331]

The minister himself functions as a cartel authority in three instances under the GWB. These are all cases where direct political responsibility for a decision was thought desirable. The minister may grant permission for a cartel that does not qualify under any of the other permission norms, "if in an exceptional case, the restriction on competition is necessary for more important reasons of the entire economy generally and for the general welfare" (§ 8 I). The minister has hardly ever exercised this authority.[332] The minister is authorized to intervene to direct changes in export cartels if a cartel "substantially affects outweighing export interests of the Federal Republic of Germany" (§ 12 II No. 2 in connection with §§ 6 I, 44 I No. 2). Finally, when the Federal Cartel Authority prohibits a merger, the minister may overrule that decision and permit the merger, "if in a particular case the restriction on competition is offset by advantages for the economy generally resulting from the merger or the merger is justified by an overriding public interest" (§ 24 III 1). Before the minister can approve such a merger, he must obtain an opinion of the Monopolies Commission (§ 24b V 6). The Monopolies Commission is a standing, independent body of competition experts created to monitor industrial concentration and to assist in implementation of merger and market-dominating enterprise abuse controls. Its role is purely advisory (§ 24b).

The Courts

Peculiarities of Cartel Law

The courts have major responsibilities in implementation of the GWB. They apply prohibition norms in private cases and in quasi-criminal prosecutions. They review application of all norms by administrative authorities. Relatively few judges, however, exercise these responsibilities. Cartel law questions are concentrated with just a few courts. And, while German judges are generally specialized, those charged with carrying out the GWB are specialized to an extent unusual even in German law. The effect intended by this concentration and specialization has largely been reached – de facto creation of a separate cartel law court system within the regular court system. Such a specialized system, it was hoped, would lead to uniform interpretation of the law and to an application of the law close to the technically complex factual situations arising under cartel law.[333]

Had general German law applied, decisions under the GWB would have been split among several different systems of courts and among numerous different court levels. Civil courts at either the lower district court or district court level would have been first instance for civil cases; criminal courts at the lower district level would have been first instance for quasi-criminal cases; administrative courts would have been first instance for review of administrative applications; three separate courts would have been final instance for questions of law (the civil and criminal senates of the Federal Supreme Court and the Federal Supreme Administrative Court). To avoid the danger of conflicting interpretations of the law, the GWB departs from general German law and assigns all questions to the ordinary civil courts. Moreover, it concentrates these questions with the courts of appeals.

The GWB creates special cartel law panels ("senates") at each court of appeals. These panels are first instance for quasi-criminal prosecutions and for review of administrative action. They also hear appeals on questions of both fact and law in private cases. By concentrating cartel decisions with the courts of appeals, the GWB eliminates one factual instance and expedites the eventual decision. The drafters of the GWB considered this desirable, because they felt many cartel law decisions would be important not only for the immediate participants, but "also for wide sectors of business and of the public."[334] The GWB does not stop with concentrating decisions with the 19 courts of appeals; it further promotes concentration with just some of the courts of appeals. The key position the GWB assigns the Federal Cartel Authority bestows a similar key role on the court of appeals which reviews decisions of the Federal Cartel Authority, the West Berlin *Kammergericht*. The GWB could not compel further concentration among the courts of appeals, since they are provincial courts, but does encourage it. The GWB authorizes German provinces to make one court of appeals responsible for all cartel law litigation within the province or, by interprovincial agreement, for all cartel law litigation within several provinces (§ 93). Every province that has more than one court of appeals has taken advantage of the former possibility.

The GWB continues the principles of concentration and specialization at other court levels. It creates a special panel at the Federal Supreme Court to hear all appeals from decisions of the courts of appeals in cartel law matters (§ 95). The GWB bestows exclusive first instance jurisdiction on the district courts for all private cases based on the GWB or on cartel agreements, and thus excludes the lower district courts, which would otherwise have a limited jurisdiction; it directs district court cases to the courts' chambers for trade matters (*Kammern für Handelssachen*) (§ 87). The GWB authorizes the provinces to concentrate cartel law questions with one district court in a fashion analogous to the possibility provided for the courts of appeals (§ 89). The provinces have made comparable use of this provision. At all court levels, whenever resolution of a controversy turns on a question of cartel law, the court must refer the question to the judicial and administrative authorities competent under the GWB (§ 96 II 1).

In the Federal Republic of Germany judging is a lifelong profession. German judges are career civil servants who begin service in their youth with lower courts. Service with higher courts comes as a professional advancement. German judges specialize, not only as among various different systems of civil, criminal, administrative, labor, and social courts, but also by task within individual courts. Concentration of cartel law decisions in special panels of the courts of appeals was thought to work to assure that judges deciding cartel law questions combine "great legal sophistication" with "particular insight into commercial matters."[335] By virtue of the general constitution of the various courts to which cartel law decisions are delegated, all cartel law decisions are reached by collegial courts. The courts of appeals decide in panels of three professional judges, the Federal Supreme Court in a panel of five professional judges. The chambers for trade matters of district courts decide in panels of one professional judge and two honorary merchant judges; the latter are appointed for three-year terms upon recommendation of the chambers of commerce and must be merchants or hold responsible positions in commerce.

Appeals

The key role of the courts of appeals in control of application of the GWB is apparent when the right to appeal cartel law decisions is considered. A right to comprehensive reconsideration of a legal decision is typical for German law generally[336] and perhaps is even more pronounced under the GWB than elsewhere. In every form of proceeding under the GWB, the courts of appeals have a reviewing role. In this role, the court not only reviews an already researched factual situation, but is also responsible itself to investigate. In both civil and administrative proceedings it has the detailed statement of reasons (*Begründung*) of the trial court or cartel authority justifying the findings of fact and the application of the law. From decisions of the courts of appeals, one further appeal to the cartel senate of the Federal Supreme Court is possible. This appeal is on questions of law alone; the Supreme Court is bound by the factual findings of the court of appeals. Appeal to the Supreme Court is frequent. For example, in 1978 the Supreme Court decided 26 cartel law appeals in civil matters, two in quasi-criminal cases, and four in administrative cases.[337] The particular role of the courts of appeals in control of GWB decisions varies with the procedural form employed.

Simplest is the role of the court of appeals in private cases under the GWB; here the court of appeals is the normal first level of appeal (*Berufung*) of German civil procedure. The German form of appeal known as *Berufung* is an appeal considerably broader than any American appeal. It corrects errors of fact as well as of law. A more fundamental difference from American appeal, though, is that the goal of *Berufung* is not the mere correction of error, but rather a completely new decision of the controversy through continuation and renewal of the proceedings; the introduction of new evidence is fundamentally allowed.[338] The court of appeals decides by ordinary judgment, and must itself fully carry through the subsumption required by the applicable norm.[339] In the event the trial court erred in its subsumption, the usual practice in *Berufung* is to correct the error there and not to return the case to the lower court.[340]

In quasi-criminal cases under the GWB the court of appeals has the role of a lower district court under the regulatory infractions law (OWiG). It is court of first instance. In such cases, the cartel authorities have reached a decision ordering a penalty (*Bußgeldbescheid*); this decision includes much particular information, but has no formal statement of reasons (*Begründung*).[341] Because the subject of the penalty order chooses to contest it, it has only the character of an accusation before the court of appeals.[342] The court of appeals then tries the case basically as any criminal case. The court is subject to the principle of judicial investigation and must investigate particulars of the accusation, including all elements of the *Tatbestand*. For quasi-criminal proceedings under the GWB, the court of appeals is the only judicial instance that considers factual questions.

Prosecution of quasi-criminal violations of the GWB is within the *pflichtgemäß* discretion of the cartel authorities (*Opportunitätsprinzip*). While this is the rule for regulatory infractions generally, it is a departure from the usual rule in German criminal procedure of compulsory prosecution (*Legalitätsprinzip*).[343] *Pflichtgemäß* means that discretion must be within the sense and purpose of the statute. The authorities may not arbitrarily decide to treat two similar cases differently. Should an authority decide not to issue a penalty order after initiating an investigation, it must incorporate that decision in an official act. There is, however, no action available to compel prosecution such as is available against the prosecuting attorney in ordinary criminal cases (no *Klageerzwingungsverfahren*) (§ 46 III 3 OWiG). The only recourse is to organize internal controls.[344]

In its review of administrative decisions of the cartel authorities, the court of appeals basically functions as an administrative court. The court is subject to the principle of judicial investigation and must investigate the factual situation fully without regard to the participants' submissions (§ 69 I-II).[345] The court entertains challenges not only to positive orders (*Anfechtungsbeschwerde*), but also challenges to inaction of the cartel authorities (*Verpflichtungsbeschwerde*) (§ 62 I, III).[346] While general German administrative law allows complaint to administrative courts only if a party has been injured in his rights,[347] the GWB widens the circle of those eligible and permits all participants in prior administrative proceedings to appeal cartel authority orders (§ 62 II).[348] Challenges to inaction still require, however, that the complainant have a right to official activity (§ 62 III 1). Normally, this is not the case where the cartel authorities have discretion to act.[349]

The review the court of appeals conducts of decisions of the cartel authorities is broader than the usual control of administrative action. Administrative courts check only for the legality (*Rechtmäßigkeit*) of administrative action: their review extends only to check whether there has been an overstepping of discretion (*Ermessensüberschreitung*) or an abuse of discretion (*Ermessensmißbrauch*).[350] The court of appeals, however, is authorized not only to review the legality of the cartel authorities' exercise of discretion, but also its utility (*Zweckmäßigkeit*).[351] The exact extent of this review is disputed, but is generally conceded to exceed that of normal administrative review.[352] This widened review has been said to be a kind of adjustment for the indefiniteness of GWB norms.[353] It was adopted as a compromise to avoid a proposal that the cartel authorities should function only as investigators and not decide cases themselves.[354] The GWB withdraws "the judgment of the general economic situation and development" from the court's review (§ 70 V 2). The courts of appeals are said in practice to accept utility judgments of the cartel authorities.[355] The question of the extent to which the court of appeals may substitute its discretion for that of the cartel authority should not obscure that, over and above the proofing of the application of the law, the court of appeals is charged with a thorough review of the underlying factual findings.[356] The broad mandate for review forces the cartel authorities themselves to be thorough in their investigations of the underlying facts.

DECISION MAKERS IN AMERICAN ANTITRUST LAW

A great variety of decision makers take part in the appplication of antitrust laws in the United States. In part, this is a consequence of American federalism. In contrast to German federalism, where the federal government ordinarily provides only a national superstructure and the provinces furnish the necessary substructure, in American federalism the 50 states and the federal government all have their own complete structures. Thus, for example, in every state there are separate state and federal courts and separate state and federal prosecutors. Among the states, there is much similarity, but rarely identity of institutions. For this work, it would be counterproductive to delve into all the details of these institutions. A sufficient picture of the decision makers in American antitrust law is given by consideration of the two most important – the federal courts and the Antitrust Division of the Department of Justice. Other institutions need only be identified and discussed incidentally.

The American antitrust statutes entrust their implementation in first line to the federal district courts and to the U.S.attorneys "under the direction of the Attorney General" (Sherman Act § 4, Clayton Act § 5). The courts determine private claims and government civil and criminal prosecutions. The U.S. attorneys are semi-autonomous federal prosecution offices; there is one in each of the roughly 100 federal judicial districts. The attorney general is a member of the president's cabinet and head of the Department of Justice. Only rarely, however, are U.S. attorneys responsible for originating antitrust litigation. Instead, "direction" of the attorney general has evolved into creation of a special prosecution unit for antitrust matters – the Antitrust Division. The Antitrust Division is an integral part of the Department of Justice in Washington and is headed by an assistant attorney general.[357]This evolution has not affected the role originally assigned the U.S. attorneys; the Antitrust Division remains a prosecuting organ. It investigates causes for presentation to the district courts for determination. Although the Antitrust Division probably has the most visible position in implementation of antitrust law, another federal authority has almost as visible a position – the Federal Trade Commission (FTC).[358] Originally, the FTC enforced only the Clayton Act and its own FTC Act, which prohibits "unfair methods of competition" (FTC Act § 5). The latter provision, however, was construed to reach violations of the Sherman Act as well. Unlike the Antitrust Division, the FTC adjudicates cases itself and does not present them to district courts for decision. According to American administrative law, it can impose no criminal penalties. Decisions of the FTC are reviewed by federal courts of appeals, and by the United States Supreme Court, that is to say, by the same courts which review decisions of the federal district courts.

Besides the federal antitrust authorities and the federal courts, state prosecutors and judges participate in application of antitrust law.[359] Recently, state attorneys general were authorized to sue in federal district courts for violations of the Sherman Act, which damage citizens of their states (so-called parens patria suits; Clayton Act §§ 4C-4H), and they could always sue for damages to the state government itself. Most states also have their own antitrust laws, which their attorneys general enforce in state courts. These laws vary considerably from state to state, as do the resources devoted to enforcement. In the 1970s the federal government promoted state antitrust enforcement. Decisions of state courts in enforcement of state antitrust laws are subject to federal review only by the Supreme Court, and only if a question of federal law is involved.

The discussion in this work is limited fundamentally to the federal court system and the Antitrust Division and only occasionally to state decision makers. This is not a damaging simplification, since the overwhelming majority of antitrust cases in the United States are handled within the federal court system after initiation by private parties or by the Antitrust Division. Moreover, differences between federal and state procedures tend to be more in detail and quality than in kind and nature. Omission of the FTC is more regrettable, yet justifiable for similar reasons. While the FTC has an important role in implementation of antitrust laws, the Antitrust Division tends to set the tone for enforcement. Moreover, while FTC procedure presents many peculiarities which would require explication, in relation to this work, its substance is not as different as its different terminology might suggest. The FTC works under administrative procedure, but that is not at all similar to German administrative procedure. In general, American administrative procedure has often been pressed to become more like judicial procedure. These pressures are particularly apparent in antitrust enforcement, where there have been proposals to transfer FTC decisional authority to federal district courts.[360] While such a transfer has not yet occurred, the FTC has structured itself so that in antitrust matters it now functions largely along the lines of traditional litigation. Its Bureau of Competition acts like a prosecutor, similar to the Antitrust Division. The Bureau presents cases to administrative law judges, who act like federal district judges. The differences between the two procedures are increasingly fewer; the most distinctive difference which remains is that there can be no jury in cases before administrative law judges.[361]

The Federal Courts

Judge and Jury of the Trial Court

The key decision makers of American antitrust law are the federal district courts (U.S. District Courts). They have jurisdiction for the vast majority of cases brought under the American antitrust laws: all criminal prosecutions, all private cases, and all civil suits brought by the Antitrust Division.

There is at least one, and are as many as four federal district courts in each of the 50 American states. The federal district courts are courts of general jurisdiction: each one is empowered to hear practically every kind of case which may be decided in the federal system. There is very little specialization of courts by function and practically no specialization of judges by function within this system. Antitrust law follows American law generally and largely allows the parties to determine geographically which district court hears a particular case. The plaintiff may sue the defendant wherever he can find the latter, and where the conduct took place. A similar choice of district courts is available in criminal antitrust cases, because the charge is conspiracy and prosecution can be brought wherever one act of the conspiracy took place. The plaintiff or the prosecutor can use this choice of courts to select a preferred interpretation of law of a particular appellate circuit or to pick a particular judge ("forum shopping"). The latter form of forum shopping is possible because each district court has only a handful of judges, some only one. In all of the United States, there are only about 500 federal trial judges. The district courts normally decide with only one judge. The judge may sit with or without jury. In either case, there is no direct supervision of the decision by a professional decision maker, such as is possible with a collegiate panel, where each panel member can check the other.

The typical federal judge has had a successful career as a practicing attorney. He is appointed by the president and is confirmed in office by the Senate. Political influence in that appointment, while still strong, has receded in recent years. A federal judgeship is usually the crowning point in a career; rarely does someone become a federal judge before about 38 years of age. Promotion to higher courts is not usual. Once in office, federal judges are guaranteed almost absolute autonomy. Their salaries and their positions are constitutionally guaranteed for life. They are hardly ever removed from office; removal requires the same cumbersome procedure used to remove a president, which necessitates action by both houses of Congress (impeachment). Federal judges enjoy high prestige and are usually thought to attain the highest levels of judicial competence.

The jury is a panel of laymen. The U.S. Constitution guarantees a right to trial by jury "[i]n suits at common law, where the value in controversy shall exceed twenty dollars."[362] A jury trial is provided only if a party having a right to jury trial demands one.[363] The right to trial by jury has long been recognized for antitrust cases. Nevertheless, antitrust cases have recently been the focus of an argument that certain cases are so complicated that a lay body can never properly understand them, and therefore, according to a historical argumentation, those complicated cases do not give rise to a right to trial by jury.[364]

Although only some federal cases receive trials and only a very few receive jury trials (depending upon the district, at the very most 10 to 20 percent, more likely, 5 percent), the work of the district court is colored by this ever present possibility. The possibility of a jury trial forces strict separation of factual and legal issues. When a jury is called, the jury decides all factual issues and the judge determines only legal questions. The jury is autonomous in its decision. The judge instructs the jury orally on the legal rules it is to apply, and the jury retires, to decide the case in secret as it sees fit. Every interference with jury autonomy is regarded with suspicion in the United States; for example, the English practice of the judge commenting on the evidence and even recommending a verdict is discouraged.[365] The principle of jury autonomy was established in England already in 1670 in *Bushell's Case*.[366] It is maintained fully in American criminal law, where a jury verdict of acquittal cannot be challenged, no matter how strong the evidence of the defendant's guilt. The jury is allowed to decide against the law (jury nullification).[367] In civil cases, on the other hand, the principle of jury autonomy has been modified to subject the jury to some control by the judge. When the evidence presented is overwhelming, the judge may "direct a verdict" or may enter judgment notwithstanding a contrary verdict of the jury. Such action requires the judge to conclude that, as a matter of law, no reason-able jury could have found otherwise on the evidence presented.[368]

The trial jury consists of from six to 12 laymen. The parties themselves choose the jurors from a larger array selected at random from the general populace. Jurors serve only a few days or for one case. Residence in the district, legal majority (18 years of age), and a minimal level of literacy are about the only requirements in the federal system. Recently, there have been proposals that jurors in complex cases (such as antitrust) should be held to higher educational requirements (for example, college), but these have not yet even reached the formal study stage. As it is, there are complaints that it is difficult to get any well-educated jurors, let alone a full panel.[369]

The jurors hear the case passively. They are not allowed to ask questions. It is even debated whether they should be allowed to take notes – for it is feared that the juror who takes notes will exercise an undue influence on others who do not. The jurors decide by unanimous vote, unless the parties stipulate otherwise. If the jurors are unable to reach a verdict (deadlock), the judge must order a new trial. Ordinarily, the jurors return what is called a general verdict, which furnishes no specific information or justification. It takes the form: "We the jury find for the defendant in the amount of five thousand dollars." To a very limited extent the jurors may be questioned about their verdict afterwards. It is also possible to have the jury return what is called a special verdict, that is, to give factual findings on specific questions.[370] Neither of these techniques is similar to or functions as the German statement of reasons (*Begründung*).[371] Custom, in any case, prefers the general verdict. The jurors' participation is limited to determination of liability and assessment of dollar damages; the judge makes such other determinations as are necessary to apply other remedies.

Trial by jury is thought to bring benefits such as individualization of justice, popular acceptance of legal decisions, and infusion of community values into the administration of justice. It is especially valued as a check on abuse of government power. Consequently, jury nullification is not considered a drawback, but a positive benefit. It makes imposition of a widely unpopular law practically impossible. It permits relaxing rigid legal rules in appealing circumstances without creating troublesome precedents.[372]

Appeals

Decisions of the federal district courts may be appealed to the competent federal court of appeals (U.S. Court of Appeals). There are 13 such courts in the United States; with one exception not important here, each is responsible for a particular region, consisting usually of several states. Karl Llewelyn once observed that the courts of the different regions sometimes act as if they were courts in different independent countries.[373] Each circuit (that is, the region for which each court is competent) has its own body of precedents and considers itself bound only by its own decisions. Decisions of the other circuits are considered persuasive, but are not binding authority. The courts of appeals sit in changing panels of three professional judges; there is no lay participation. Should different panels in the same circuit disagree, all the judges of the court may sit en banc to decide the issue.

Decisions of the courts of appeals may be reviewed by the U.S. Supreme Court. In most cases, Supreme Court review is possible only if the Court chooses to hear the case. It usually chooses to hear only cases that raise important legal questions or that settle questions where different circuits have interpreted the law differently. The Supreme Court has nine justices who normally all participate in decision of all cases. Consequently, the Court is able to decide only a small number of cases with full opinion, about 100 to 200 cases a year. Of these, typically about five relate to antitrust.

Although the courts of appeals and the Supreme Court decide in panels of several judges, they are not collegiate courts in the German sense. As in Germany, judges vote individually. But in the United States, where they do not agree with the decision or with the reasoning of the majority, they frequently publish their own separate opinions (dissenting and concurring opinions). Such dissenting opinions are particularly common in antitrust cases.

The issue narrowing of the trial court proceedings, discussed in Chapter 6, is still more a feature of appeals. Courts of appeals consider only those issues presented to them. Good appellate advocacy demands – the Supreme Court recently reminded American lawyers – "winnowing out weaker arguments on appeal and focusing on one central issue if possible, or at most on a few key issues."[374] The choice of which issue to emphasize belongs to the attorneys, not to the courts. Consequently, appellate judges do not select the material on which they base their decisions. The appellate courts are, in effect, forced to choose between two competing alternatives offered them by the adversary attorneys, at least insofar as their decisions are based on factual rather than on legal arguments.

Appeal in the federal system is limited to questions of law. In the German sense there is only *Revision*; there is not "*Berufung*." Usual appeals are challenges to decisions of pretrial motions, evidentiary rulings at trial, and proposed jury instructions. Factual determinations may be challenged indirectly through devices such as challenges to denial of a motion for directed verdict. A motion for directed verdict asks the judge to decide that the evidence the court has heard so clearly supports one side that, as a matter of law, no reasonable jury could decide other than for the movant. In an appeal from denial of such a motion, the appellate court reviews the trial record to determine whether the evidence presented was so one-sided that no reasonable jury could find against the movant. Because jury verdicts are usually general verdicts, the appellate court ordinarily has no factual findings to review. When the case has been tried to a judge alone, instead of a jury, there may be such findings. Ordinarily, even in those cases, the judge does not justify his findings in the fashion of a German judgment; indeed, he may well simply adopt findings submitted by the lawyers. Nevertheless, appellate review in such cases is not much different. The appellate court reviews the trial transcripts (which are verbatim) to see if the judge's findings are justified. If the court finds substantial error, it usually must return the case to the trial court for further action. The appellate court cannot itself call witnesses and has only limited possibilities to correct errors itself. Consequently, appellate courts do not lightly overturn trial courts' factual findings. This reluctance to reverse factual findings extends not only to jury findings, but also to judicial findings. Federal Rule of Civil Procedure 52(a) (3) states the standard for overturning judicial findings of fact: "Findings of fact shall not be set aside unless clearly erroneous, and due regard shall be given to the opportunity of the trial court to judge the credibility of the witnesses." Mirjan Damaška has observed that the inscrutability of the jury verdict has made the Anglo-American appeal something other than a review of the trial court's decision: "what is actually reviewed is the propriety of the material submitted to the decision maker for decision rather than his 'correct' use of the material."[375]

The Antitrust Division

Role as Prosecutor

The Antitrust Division of the Department of Justice is the only federal agency exclusively specialized in antitrust law and has the most visible role in antitrust enforcement. Its role is that of an American prosecutor. The American prosecutor functions very differently from his German counterpart.[376] In the Federal Republic of Germany, the prosecutor is supposed to have little discretion: When a certain minimum level of suspicion is reached, he *must* prosecute (*Legalitätsprinzip*). Controls exist to insure fulfillment of this duty. In the United States, on the other hand, the prosecutor is assumed necessarily to have substantial and uncontrolled discretion. He decides when to investigate. He decides whether to prosecute. When he does prosecute, he is largely free to withdraw the prosecution or modify the charge until final judgment. The American prosecutor reaches these decisions mostly in secret[377] and subject to few controls. At no stage must he formally justify his decisions. Practically the only substantial legal control he is subject to is that his positive decision to prosecute must rest upon well-founded suspicion (probable cause). His negative decisions not to investigate, not to prosecute, or to settle or withdraw a prosecution once brought are not controlled and need not be justified. A victim unhappy with the prosecutor's failure to act has no action comparable to the German action to compel prosecution (*Klageerzwingungsverfahren*). A recent civil antitrust case is a dramatic example of the prosecutor's power to drop a case: After 13 years of pretrial and trial work, the Antitrust Division withdrew its monopolization case against IBM as being "without merit."[378] A government prosecution, whether civil or criminal, is treated largely as the "prosecutor's case." It is a party process; in German terminology, it is completely dominated by the principles of party presentation and party control.

In a critique of prosecutorial discretion Kenneth Culp Davis observed that "Uncontrolled discretionary power of prosecutors is simply assumed in America."[379] He found deep skepticism that it could be controlled, and an "almost universal" conviction of its necessity. He encountered a general belief that "The prosecuting power intrinsically involves broad discretion because (1) in the nature of things all law can't be enforced, (2) the prosecutor has to interpret uncertain statutory provisions, and (3) the prosecutor has to exercise discretion in deciding whether the evidence is sufficient."[380]

Although the prosecutor's decision is largely uncontrolled, the prosecutor himself is subject to some controls. Most prosecutorial offices are organized hierarchically at the local level. The head of the office (called variously, the district attorney, the prosecuting attorney, or the U.S. attorney) is usually politically responsible. In the individual states most district attorneys are elected. In the federal system U.S. attorneys are appointed politically by each new president. The popular and political nature of this control affects the public's expectations of the prosecutor. The public looks to the prosecutor as a public official responsible for the maintenance of order. In the public's eyes, that often is couched in terms such as: What is your win/loss record?, that is, How many of your prosecutions resulted in convictions? The public expects the prosecutor will neither enforce unpopular laws nor will enforce popular laws unjustly or unwisely. The prosecutor who fulfills these expectations might be seen, in part, to exercise by proxy the jury's power of nullification; by deciding not to prosecute in cases where a jury would not convict, the prosecutor saves the public the expense of a trial. Such discretionary power, of course, makes it just as possible for the prosecutor to nullify a law on his own initiative.

Critics of uncontrolled prosecutorial discretion have not asked a question suggested by the subject of this work: Is there a connection between broad prosecutorial discretion and the American legal method of issue narrowing? In the Federal Republic of Germany, the prosecutor must prosecute whenever a minimum level of suspicion is reached. It is then the court's duty to investigate the charges fully. Before the court may order punishment, it must subsume the case under the *Tatbestand* of the corresponding norm. It must consider all the elements of the *Tatbestand.* The American court, on the other hand, considers only those issues the parties choose to contest. Adversary presentation makes presentation and consideration of uncontested issues wasteful and foolish. But if the parties are to control what issues are contested, the prosecutor as a party must himself have at least some discretion. That is the cost of giving him power to shape the issues. This may explain why prosecutorial discretion seems so natural in common law countries while it is anathema on the Continent.[381]

The advocate's role in shaping the issues may also help explain the schizophrenia which afflicts American lawyers in general and American prosecutors in particular. Are they advocates for the parties who retain them (cynically, hired guns), or are they officers of the court (truth seekers)? To some extent, this dilemma is present wherever private representation is permitted, but it is stronger in the United States than in the Federal Republic of Germany. The party to a law suit cannot be expected to want other than to win. The adversary system demands that his attorney work for that victory. The American prosecutor is subject to the same pressure of party representation (What is your conviction ratio?). He knows that his adversary wants to get the accused "off." Give the lawyers a role in issue shaping, and the lawyer who wants to win will be loath to concede any point and will be anxious to raise every issue to his client's benefit. If one party happens to be better positioned to contest an issue – perhaps he has better information or he has more resources – is the lawyer who fails to take that advantage true to his client? If he doesn't, he risks loss of the case and causes his client additional expenses. (In the United States the parties normally bear their own legal expenses.) In England, this problem of split allegiances is addressed by the system of barristers. The lawyers who present the case are not directly retained by the client, but are chosen by an intermediary (the solicitor). The barristers have no legal right to payment from the party whose case they present. They are in fact officers of the court. In the United States, on the other hand, the trial lawyer is directly retained by the client. His fee may even depend on his victory (contingent fee).[382]

The Antitrust Division is subject to these same tensions. It is expected to maintain competitive order – to enforce the law. Yet, it should not enforce the law unreasonably. But antitrust law is often vague. How far should the Antitrust Division reason analogically from a particular precedent? When a particular precedent is of dubious economic validity, should the Antitrust Division ignore it? Whose view of economics should the Antitrust Division take? If a given rule of antitrust law provides a simplification which helps prove the case (that is, helps the Division "win its case"), should the Division take advantage of it? Former Assistant Attorney General Donald Turner created a stir when he said the Antitrust Division should not bring every case it *could* win, but only those cases it *should* win.[383] Insofar as the Antitrust Division follows the course recommended by Turner, however, it does so as an American prosecutor – largely informally, secretly, and uncontrolled. In another context, Lawrence Sullivan has observed:

> But if a different and more sophisticated set of norms are used in deciding what industries ought to be challenged than those proposed to the court as governing its decision, much of the value in what a system of law provides is lost. The agency, in refining its norms, in developing a factual basis and in drawing inferences, will be wholly insulated from the parties. What may be the real decisions will be made without party participation. The presentation in court becomes something of a charade, where the norms which the Division presses on the court are far more sweeping than those it manipulates by itself.[384]

If the Antitrust Division must compensate for failure in the law, where should it find the measure of its responsibility?

Recently the American Congress has taken steps to control prosecutorial discretion in antitrust cases. Since 1974 it has required federal district courts to review civil consent settlements reached by the Antitrust Division (consent judgments) to see that they are in the public interest. The Antitrust Division must file so-called competitive impact statements with the courts in response to which public comments are invited.[385] The extent of this control remains to be seen. The traditional passive role of the American judge may, however, make it difficult for this control to be extensive. In declining to interfere with a consent judgment, Court of Appeals for the Ninth Circuit recently commented:

> The balancing of competing social and political interests affected by a proposed antitrust consent decree must be left, in the first instance, to the discretion of the Attorney General. The court's role in protecting the public interest is one of insuring that the government has not breached its duty to the public in consenting to the decree. The court is required to determine not whether a particular decree is the one that will best serve society, but whether the settlement is "within the reaches of the public interest."[386]

The Court's language is reminiscent of German terminology: The review it calls for seems similar to the review ordinarily conducted by German administrative courts and not the wider review of German cartel law. While it can review for an abuse of discretion without an immediate standard, it can review for an overstepping of discretion only if it has an explicit standard. What will set the limit of the discretion of the Antitrust Division? The legal method of American antitrust law is the common law method of analogy. Analogy sets no limit, only a direction; it forces the Antitrust Division to make new law to deal with new situations.

There have been no significant efforts to alter the Antitrust Division's role as prosecutor.[387] This is not surprising, since such a proposal probably would not be successful. Such a proposal may be doomed, not so much because of contemporary "deregulation" rhetoric, but because Americans are suspicious of government and prefer to trust in adversary procedure for protection. The repeated attempts to "reform" the FTC, which would take away its decision authority and make it function as a prosecutor, is an example of this preference.[388] Indeed, the role of the Antitrust Division as a prosecutor has been seen not as a weakness, but as a strength. To it is attributed the Division's relative "cleanness." Where other agencies charged with regulating American industry are seen to have been "captured" by those very industries, the Antitrust Division has maintained its independence.[389]

Without departing from its role as prosecutor, the Antitrust Division has occasionally taken on other roles as advocate for competition and as coordinator of antitrust enforcement. Under some assistant attorneys general, the Antitrust Division has been particularly active in these roles. In 1978 the then assistant attorney general reported to Congress that the Division's mission was "to make competition work throughout the American economy" and called attention to these other roles.[390] As advocate of competition, the Antitrust Division comments on proposed legislation affecting competition. To further this and other roles, the Antitrust Division has sought to develop economic expertise. Nothing comparable to the Federal Cartel Authority's biennial reports has ever resulted.

The Antitrust Division has had only limited success in its attempts to coordinate antitrust enforcement. In these efforts, the Antitrust Division largely has had to work informally and without statutory authorization. The Antitrust Division maintains semiformal contacts with the FTC to avoid duplication of investigations. It administers federal grants supporting state enforcement of antitrust laws. The state authorities are not, however, required to notify the Antitrust Division of their cases.

The attempts of the Antitrust Division to guide the application of antitrust law flounder on two obstacles which make a uniform coordination difficult, if not fully foreclose it. Most provisions of American antitrust law can be enforced by private parties. It cannot be expected that the Antitrust Division will ever be able to direct these parties. Still more serious, the Antitrust Division has few possibilities to influence the federal judges who actually decide these private antitrust cases. The procedure of antitrust cases is a party procedure. If the Antitrust Division is not a party in a particular case, it can do little toinfluence policy decisions made in the course of that case. Insofar as the Antitrust Division can exercise some influence, it is restricted to legal questions. In the appellate courts, the Antitrust Division may, with the permission of the court, submit its comments on the law applicable to the case; permission is usually granted. Recently, the Antitrust Division has sought to extend this practice to the trial courts.[391] Still, here too its influence would be limited to legal questions.

Organization of the Antitrust Division

The Antitrust Division is organized hierarchically. Individual sections of ten to 50 lawyers conduct investigations and trials. All important decisions, such as to bring a prosecution, are subject to approval by the head of the section, the director of the Office of Operations (which oversees the sections), and the assistant attorney general in charge of the Antitrust Division.[392] The assistant attorney general is the operating head of the Antitrust Division and controls its prosecutorial discretion. Nevertheless, the assistant attorney general is only on the third level of the hierarchy of the Department of Justice and his decisions may, on occasion, be reversed by the attorney general. Accordingly, the assistant attorney general usually discusses questions of particular political interest with the attorney general. Although the attorney general is not legally limited in his control of the Antitrust Division, he does not interfere in the operation of the Antitrust Division frequently. When he does, he usually intervenes at the point of the decision to bring the prosecution. In the Carter administration, for example, the attorney general stopped the Antitrust Division from challenging a merger of two steel companies; the Antitrust Division section had recommended prosecution and the assistant attorney general had approved it. In overruling the Antitrust Division, the attorney general was not required to justify his decision formally. In this particular case, the attorney general apparently decided to allow the merger out of concern for employment in the affected geographical areas.

The assistant attorney general in charge of the Antitrust Division is a political appointee. He changes at least as frequently as the administration. In the last quarter century the typical assistant attorney general has served about two years. His deputy assistant attorneys general (presently four) are similarly political appointees and serve at his pleasure. Only exceptionally has any of these officials had experience within the Antitrust Division, although commonly they have had professional experience as practitioners or teachers in the antitrust field. The influence the assistant attorney general has on the Antitrust Division during his short tenure is judged variously. Some see him as unable to control the Antitrust Division, in particular, in its tendencies toward a prosecutorial mentality. My own perception is that, despite short tenure, he has a major impact on the general direction of the Antitrust Division. His control over the Antitrust Division's discretion and the uncertain contours of substantive law make it possible for him to play the key role in shaping antitrust policy, to the extent that anyone can take that role in the United States.

The Antitrust Division has several hundred lawyers and several dozen economists organized in litigating and staff sections, most of whom are located in Washington. The lawyers are organized in investigating and staff sections; the economists are segregated in their own section. The highest career civil service position in the Antitrust Division is director of the Office of Operations. The next highest positions are the section chiefs of the sections and the few regional field offices. Each of them has one or more assistant chiefs. The remaining lawyers, with few exceptions, are designated trial attorneys. Richard Posner has said the Antitrust Division's trial lawyers "tend to be young or mediocre, or to be zealots."[393] His assessment is perhaps one third right. The Antitrust Division's attorneys tend to be young. While the Antitrust Division has had success in the past in attracting some of what are perceived to be the nation's best law graduates (that is, with high marks at prestigious schools), it has had less success in retaining them. Service of less than five years in the Antitrust Division is common – service of more than ten years, unusual. Since the United States does not have a practical apprentice period for lawyers, this means the Antitrust Division loses attorneys just as they begin to develop experience. Since the assistant attorney general and his deputies themselves are usually with the Division no more than two years, continuity in antitrust enforcement is brought largely by a small group of dedicated section chiefs and experienced staff attorneys. However, these lawyers have relatively little control over the actual policy decisions.

8

Summary and Outlook

I. American antitrust law is widely criticized for uncertainty, cumbersome application, and economic oversimplification. Although German cartel law borrows much of its substance from American law, it is widely accepted and encounters no criticism comparable to that received by its American counterpart.

The fundamental criticism of American antitrust law is twofold: it is that the law is bad as law and bad as policy. It is thought to be bad as law in that it does not meet minimum standards of certainty and ease of application required by the Rule of Law. It is thought to be bad as economic policy in that it is often neither coherent or consistent, nor in accord with sound economic analysis.

The thesis of this work is that many of the problems that afflict American antitrust law should be recognized to be problems of legal method. German and American antitrust laws are judged differently not so much because they diverge widely in substance, but because they differ greatly in method. In part, these differences in methods are characteristic of differences typical of German and American law generally. But in antitrust law, characteristic differences achieve particular significance because of a difference peculiar to antitrust law: antitrust law requires constant public policy decisions.

II. Public policy decisions create particular problems for protection of the legal certainty interest of the Rule of Law. The Rule of Law demands a certain rigidity in law in order to permit the law to guide the citizen and to protect him from arbitrary government action. In both the United States and the Federal Republic of Germany it is common to recognize that there is greater danger to the Rule of Law, when a legal rule is relaxed for the sake of public policy than when a rule is relaxed for the sake of justice. A greater danger results because public policy decisions pit individual interest directly against community interest and can unite in one decision maker the functions of determining community interest and exercising the resulting governmental authority.

III. Both German and American antitrust laws frequently relax rigid legal rules to require the decision maker applying the law to make public policy decisions. One such kind of public policy decision which occurs frequently is to make an economic judgment of effect on competition. American antitrust law requires public policy decisions, for example, in application of the so-called rule of reason to restraints of trade, in evaluation of monopolization charges, and in measurement of the economic effect of mergers. German cartel law requires public policy decisions, for example, in granting exemptions to the general ban on cartel agreements, in control of abuses by market-dominating enterprises, and in evaluating mergers.

IV. When it is not possible to bind positively legal decisions, that is, when a decision maker is permitted a value judgment such as a policy decision, the interests expressed by the Rule of Law in orientation and protection of the individual demand that these legal decisions be at least limited. The very different approaches American and German antitrust law take to binding the decision maker in part explain the relatively different judgments of the two laws.

Precedent is the principal means of limiting legal decisions in American law. Precedent rules themselves are narrowly circumscribed factually and have claim to bind only inferior courts. However, they do limit all courts by creating a network of "interstitial limits," that is, points from which judges develop analogies, but contrary to which judges cannot easily decide. Within the freedom allowed by these "interstitial limits" judges are to guide their decisions by considerations of equity.

Precedents are often ineffective as limits on American antitrust policy decisions. These decisions are frequently factual and therefore not directly subject to the narrow rules developed by precedent. Because antitrust policy decisions often deal with complex situations, development of "interstitial limits" is retarded. Moreover, the primacy of antitrust policy permits its policy decisions to override potential "interstitial limits" from other areas of law. Finally, policy, not equity, is to guide otherwise unlimited antitrust decisions, and since there is less likelihood of consensus in matters of policy as compared to matters of equity, there is reduced predictability.

Other common law limits, effective in other areas of legal decision, function poorly or not at all as limits on American antitrust policy decisions. The restriction of decision to the judicial function of dispute resolution, which was once rigorously enforced by a rigid formulary system, does not exist in antitrust law, where any market participant is allowed to claim almost any practice as potentially anticompetitive. The old common law limitation on the potential remedies a judge can order was abolished with the merger of law and equity courts and cannot limit antitrust policy decisions. New limits that are often imposed by statute are not imposed by the antitrust statutes, which are little more than authorizations to develop a judge-made law of trade restraint.

Statute is the principal means of limiting legal decisions in German law. Before a decision maker can order a particular legal result, he must find an authorizing statutory norm and must subsume the facts of the particular case under all the elements of the *Tatbestand* of the authorizing statute. Room for value judgments arises as a choice between applicable statutes, or when an authorizing statute utilizes one or more indefinite legal concepts or explicitly grants discretion to choose among possible legal results.

German cartel law provides many limits on antitrust policy decisions in the statute which authorizes value judgments. While the statute frequently utilizes indefinite legal concepts to describe particular conduct or situations, and often explicitly grants discretion to make policy choices, at the same time as it thus unbinds decisions it places other negative limits on these decisions. In particular, it circumscribes *who* may order *what* measure against *whom, when.* The most important such negative limits are the restriction of policy decisions to the competence of administrative authorities and the limitation of the effect of their decisions to the future.

V. German cartel law generally assigns antitrust policy decisions to administrative authorities, while it gives culpability questions to the judiciary. It does this by creating three separate types of norm: prohibition norms, permission norms, and intervention norms. When a policy decision is required, it is usually incorporated in application of a permission or of an intervention norm. These two types of norms are applied exclusively by administrative authorities. Applications of these norms can have only future effect. Where an equity judgment is required, such as of individual culpability, this judgment is usually made in application of a prohibition norm. Prohibition norms can be applied with repressive effect and with effect for past action, but only where there is a possibility of full judicial proceedings.

The separate treatment of policy and equity decisions assures that the two types of decisions are not regularly reached in the same proceeding. It permits policy decisions to be made with the principal concern for the policy effect unencumbered by extraneous concerns of individual fairness. On the other hand, judgments of individual culpability can be reached unencumbered by possibly conflicting public policy concerns. The separation of the two types of judgment thus contributes both to heightened rule of law security and improved policy making. A similar effect is promoted by restriction of public policy decisions to future effect.

This separation in German cartel law of equity and policy decisions is not in all respects complete and has moreover certain disadvantages. However, these difficulties appear to be relatively insubstantial in comparison to the difficulties that result from lack of a comparable separation of policy and equity judgments in American antitrust law. American antitrust law makes no real separation of legal sanction and applicable norms; it has no separation of past- and future-directed legal orders. As a result, in American antitrust law any given attempt to apply an antitrust norm is apt to include both equity and policy judgments; the making of one of these judgments often deleteriously affects the outcome of the other.

The difficulties of this mixing of policy and equity decisions in application of American antitrust law are exacerbated by the uniform treatment of all policy decisions in American antitrust law as judicial judgments. As judicial judgments, American antitrust policy decisions have res judicata effect. German cartel law policy decisions, on the other hand, are incorporated in administrative acts and do not acquire res judicata effect. Thus German cartel law policy decisions are more flexible and permit temporizing solutions more easily than do American antitrust policy decisions.

VI. Just as the different methods of binding the decision maker have affected the relative legal certainty and quality of policy decisions in German and American antitrust law, so too have the differing methods of application of the law.

In American antitrust law the parties, and not the decision maker, are principally responsible for application of the law. Together they agree, or under compulsion of a judge, are directed to agree on making one issue, or a handful, the point or points that decide the controversy between them. The parties fully investigate these points and present their version of them to a passive decision maker. Public policy issues decided in this fashion are likely to be poorly decided if the parties appearing before the court do not represent the public interest well. If the parties are unevenly matched, their presentation may be skewed.

Public policy decisions in American antitrust call for economic investigations, which require considering many different interrelated points. The litigation system, however, demands a strict limitation of the proceedings to a few decisive points. Otherwise, the parties cannot present their case. There is an inherent antinomy in common law methods of law application and the making of antitrust policy decisions. Adversary presentation demands issue narrowing, but issue narrowing can lead to excessively simplified economic policy decisions.

German legal methods have no issue narrowing in the American sense. The decision maker is charged with applying the law. He must determine that every element of the *Tatbestand* is present. Moreover, the decision maker is in charge of the taking of evidence. In German cartel law when application of the law requires public policy decisions, the decision maker is endowed with the tools to carry on an investigation. The principles of official control and judicial investigation apply. The decision maker is not limited to presentations of parties, but must investigate himself.

Nevertheless, public policy decisions in German cartel law have created significant problems for subsumption. The use of indefinite legal concepts is so common that the usual method of binding decision to statute is not always effective to control and guide decision. However, other means are used to better control cartel law policy decisions and to make them more predictable.

VII. One means of enhancing predictability is to provide decision makers who are more predictable, even when the law cannot predetermine a particular solution. The decision makers are endowed with attributes which enhance their predictability. Such enhancement of predictability is possible, because in German cartel law who the decision maker is is largely determined by the statute. American antitrust policy decision makers often do not share these attributes of predictability, and even when they do, because who the decision maker will be is often unforeseeable, the built-in uncertainty in the law is not relieved. As a result, there should be no surprise that such widely different judgments are reached as to compliance with the Rule of Law and the degree of policy efficacy of the antitrust laws of the two countries.

The decision makers of German cartel law are largely centralized, coordinated, and collegiate. They are usually specialized and professionalized. In short, they are bureaucratic. In any particular case, the more likely the particular decision involved is a policy decision, the more pronounced are these characteristics, and the closer is the decision maker to political responsibility. In contrast, the decision makers of American antitrust law are not centralized, not coordinated, and not collegiate. They are less specialized and less professionalized than their German counterparts. They are not bureaucratic and are not subject to political responsibility.

The extra-legal justification for unbounded decisions under the two laws varies substantially. American law relies on the neutrality of the fact finder and a guarantee that those presenting the case fully argue their positions to justify such unbounded decision. The decision maker may, as a consequence, deliver a simple judgment, one way or another, without explanation. In a simple case, such methods can be satisfactory. Their efficacy in complex cases is, however, dubious. German cartel law, on the other hand, relies on the fact finder's rational argumentation to justify the fact-finder's otherwise legally unbounded decision.

Because policy decisions in the Federal Republic of Germany are subject to a high measure of centralization, who will make a given policy decision is quite predictable, even when the content of that decision is not. A workable measure of predictability may be achieved, insofar as the behavior of the decision maker is predictable for reasons external to the law itself. Such predictability is furthered by bureaucratic coordination of decision makers, by professionalization of decision makers, and by the requirement that every decision have a formal statement of reasons (*Begründung*). These organizational controls tend to promote a consistent, and therefore more predictable course of antitrust policy decisions.

In American antitrust law, who will make important policy decisions is often entirely unpredictable. That decision maker, as likely as not, may be a complete novice who is making an antitrust policy decision for the first time. And yet, that decision maker, who is not controlled by the law, is also not controlled by any superior authority or by any measure of political responsibility. The only basis for predictability of such decision may be a very vague and very limited consensus as to what constitutes a desirable public policy. Moreover, no written or oral explanation of this decision may be necessary. As a consequence, the cautious lawyer must anticipate the most irrational, least justifiable of policy decisions imaginable.

VIII. What is the outlook for American antitrust law? Given the legal and political systems within which law is created in the United States, it is probably unlikely that an awareness of the methods problems will occur. Moreover, if the serious mismatch between the legal methods employed and the tasks required of them in antitrust law were widely recognized, the majority response would apt to be similar to that of Robert Bork, who suggests, not that the legal system should be changed, but that less should be asked of the legal system.[394] Legal methods are so deeply ingrained in the legal system, while alternatives are so little known in depth, that substantial changes in legal methods are not readily envisioned, and are even less readily accomplished.

Still, an increased awareness of legal methods can be hoped for. From that standpoint, the foregoing work suggests yet another conclusion: A choice of legal methods should recognize whether policy or equity goals are to predominate in application of the law. In particular, the quite different experiences of the United States and the Federal Republic of Germany with the implementation of antitrust law suggest limitations on the use of judge-made law. While deficiencies in legislation or in the political system may require resort sometimes to judge-made policy decisions, this work suggests that it is not desirable, as a general rule, to place judges in such a predicament. This work, too, confirms Esser's observation that "The equity of the individual case, built on an optimal investigation of the facts, is an indispensable, indeed according to Anglo-Saxon conviction, is the only workable direction for a reasonable judge-made law."[395] Where the positive law cannot deliver a demonstrable, or at least defensible solution, then the judge is usually better guided by ideas of justice than by policy considerations. Moreover, policy decisions can ordinarily be expected to be better made when they are recognized as such, are made by institutions created to make policy decisions, and are reached by decision makers who can appeal to political responsibility as a basis for their decisions.[396]

Bibliography

ALLEN, Carleton Kemp: Law in the Making, 7th ed., Oxford: Oxford University Press, 1964.

AREEDA, Phillip and TURNER, Donald F.: Antitrust Law, 6 vols., Boston-Toronto: Little, Brown and Company, 1978-1980.

ARNOLD, Thurman: The Bottlenecks of Business, New York: Reynal and Hitchcock, 1940 (cited: Bottlenecks).

___: Trial by Combat and the New Deal, in: 47 Harvard L. Rev. 913-47 (1934) (cited: Trial by Combat).

BACHOF, Otto: Beurteilungsspielraum, Ermessen und unbestimmter Rechtsbegriff im Verwaltungsrecht, in: JZ 1955, 97-102, reprinted in: BACHOF; Wege zum Rechtsstaat, 154-71, Königstein/Ts.: Athenäum Verlag GmbH, 1979 (cited according to reprint).

BÄHR, Peter et al.: Zur Reform des Rechts der Wettbewerbsbeschränkungen (common statement of 15 Neoliberals), in: Wettbewerb als Aufgabe, Nach zehn Jahren Gesetz gegen Wettbewerbsbeschränkungen, 5-28, Bad Homburg: Verlag Gehlen, 1968.

BAKER, Donald I.: To Indict or Not to Indict, Prosecutorial Discretion in Sherman Act Enforcement, in: 63 Cornell L. Rev. 405 (1978).

BAKER, J. H.: An Introduction to English Legal History, 2nd ed., London: Butterworth & Co., Ltd., 1979.

BARBIER, Hans: "Bewährtes Instrument mit Schönheitsfehlern," in: Süddeutsche Zeitung, No. 170/30 W, July 28, 1982, p. 4.

BAUMBACH, Adolf and HEFERMEHL, Wolfgang: Wettbewerbs- und Warenzeichenrecht, Kommentar, 7th ed., München-Berlin: C. H. Beck'sche Verlagsbuchhandlung, 1956.

BAYLSON, Michael M.: Narrowing Issues in Antitrust Cases, in: 48 Antitrust L.J. 705-41 (1980).

BENISCH, Werner: Kooperationsfibel, 4th ed., Bergisch-Gladbach: Heider-Verlag, 1973 (with addendum 1976).

BENKENDORFF, Gerhard: Nochmals: Rechtskontrolle der Verfügungen der Kartellbehörden durch die Gerichte (§ 70 Abs. 4 GWB), in: WuW 1958, 740-50 (cited: Rechtskontrolle).

BOK, Derek C.: Section 7 of the Clayton Act and the Merging of Law and Economics, in: 74 Harvard L. Rev. 226-355 (1960).

BORK, Robert H.: The Antitrust Paradox – A Policy at War with Itself, New York: Basic Books, 1978 (cited: Paradox).

___: The Rule of Reason and the Per Se Concept: Price Fixing and Market Division, in: 74 Yale L.J. 775-847 and 75 Yale L.J. 373-473 (1966) (cited: Rule of Reason).

BORKIN, Joseph and WELSH, Charles A., with an Introduction by ARNOLD, Thurman: Germany's Master Plan, New York: Duell, Sloan and Pearce, 1943.

BROSE, Claus-Detlev and HELMCKE, Horst: Zur Kollision von Kartellzivilprozeß (§ 90 GWB) und Auskunftsverfahren (§ 46 GWB), in: WuW 1981, 845-52.

BUNTE, Hermann-Josef: Vertrauensschutz und Verwirklichung im Kartellrecht, in: BB 1980, 1073-81.

CALABRESI, Guido: A Common Law for the Age of Statutes, Cambridge/Mass.-London: Harvard University Press, 1982.

CARDOZO, Benjamin N.: The Nature of the Judicial Process, New Haven: Yale University Press, 1921.

CLARK, Charles E.: Handbook of the Law of Code Pleading, 2nd ed., St. Paul: West Publishing Co., 1947.

COHEN, Morris R.: Law and the Social Order, 1933, reprint, New Brunswick-London: Transaction Books, 1982.

CORWIN, Edward S.: The Passing of Dual Federalism, in: 36 Virginia L. Rev. 1-23 (1950).

CROSS, Rupert: Precedent in English Law, 3d ed., Oxford: Oxford University Press, 1977.

DAMAŠKA, Mirjan: Presentation of Evidence and Fact Finding Precision, in: 123 U. Pennsylvania L. Rev. 1083-1106 (1975) (cited: Presentation of Evidence).

___: Structures of Authority and Comparative Criminal Procedure, in: 84 Yale L.J. 480-544 (1975) (cited: Structures of Authority).

DAVIS, Kenneth Culp: Administrative Law Text, 3d ed., St. Paul: West Publishing Co., 1972.

___: Discretionary Justice – A Preliminary Inquiry, Baton Rouge: Louisiana State University Press, 1969 (cited: Discretionary Justice).

DIETZE, Gottfried: Kant und der Rechtsstaat, Tübingen: J. C. B. Mohr, 1982.

DWORKIN, Ronald: Taking Rights Seriously, Cambridge/Mass.: Harvard University Press, 1977 (with addendum 1978).

EBEL, Wilhelm: Geschichte der Gesetzgebung in Deutschland, Göttingen: Verlag Otto Schwartz & Co., 1958.

EMMERICH, Volker: Kartellrecht, 4th ed., München: C. H. Beck'sche Verlagsbuchhandlung, with addendum 1980 (cited: Kartellrecht).

___: Die Zuläßigkeit der Kooperation von Unternehmen auf Grund des reformierten GWB, Tübingen: J. C. B. Mohr, 1974 (cited: Kooperation).

ENGISCH, Karl: Einführung in das juristische Denken, 8th ed., Stuttgart-Berlin-Köln-Mainz: Verlag W. Kohlhammer, 1984.

ENNECCERUS, Ludwig and NIPPERDEY, Hans Carl: Allgemeiner Teil des bürgerlichen Rechts, Ein Lehrbuch, 2 vols., 14th ed., Tübingen: J. C. B. Mohr, 1952.

ERICHSEN, Hans-Uwe and MARTENS, Wolfgang (eds.): Allgemeines Verwaltungsrecht, 6th ed., Berlin-New York: Walter de Gruyter & Co., 1984.

ESSER, Josef: Grundsatz und Norm, Tübingen: J. C. B. Mohr, 1956 (cited: Grundsatz).

___: Not und Gefahren des Revisionsrechts, in: JZ 1962, 513-17, reprinted in: RÖLLECKE, Gerd (ed.): Zur Problematik der Höchstrichterlichen Entscheidung, 162-78, Darmstadt: Wissenschaftliche Buchgesellschaft, 1982 (cited according to reprint: Not).

EUCKEN, Walter: Grundlagen der Nationalökonomie, 2nd ed., Godesberg: Verlag Helmut Küpper, 1947 (cited: Grundlagen).

___: Grundsätze der Wirtschaftspolitik, 2nd ed., Tübingen-Zürich: J. C. B. Mohr and Polygraphischer Verlag, 1955 (cited: Grundsätze).

FIKENTSCHER, Wolfgang: Die deutsche Kartellrechtswissenschaft 1945-1954, in: WuW 1955, 201-29 (cited: Kartellrechtswissenschaft).

___: Deutsches Wirtschaftsrecht (Wirtschaftsrecht, vol. 2), München: C. H. Beck'sche Verlagsbuchhandlung, 1983 (cited: Wirtschaftsrecht).

___: Methoden des Rechts in vergleichender Darstellung, 5 vols., Tübingen: J. C. B. Mohr, 1975-1977 (cited: Methoden).

___: Die neuere Entwicklung des amerikanischen Wettbewerbsrechts und der deutsche Kartellgesetzentwurf, in: ZHR, vol. 117 (1955), 1-40 (cited: Entwicklung).

___: Eine Theorie der Fallnorm als Grundlage von Kodex- und Fallrecht (code law and case law), ZfRV, vol. 21 (1980), 161-74 (cited: Theorie).

FISCHER, Robert: Die Weiterbildung des Rechts durch die Rechtsprechung, Karlsruhe: Verlag C. F. Müller, 1971.

FORTSTHOFF, Ernst: Lehrbuch des Verwaltungsrechts – Allgemeiner Teil, 10th ed., München: C. H. Beck'sche Verlagsbuchhandlung, 1973.

FRANK, Jerome: Courts on Trial: Myth and Reality in American Justice, Princeton: Princeton University Press, 1950 (cited: Courts).

___: Law and the Modern Mind, New York: Brentano's, Inc., 1930, reprint, Gloucester/Mass.: Peter Smith, 1970 (cited: Law).

FRANKEL, Marvin E.: Partisan Justice, New York: Hill and Wang, 1980.

FRANKFURTER, Felix: Some Reflections on the Reading of Statutes, in: 47 Columbia L. Rev. 527-46 (1947).

FULLER: The Adversary System, in BERMAN, Harold (ed.): Talks on American Law, 34-47, 2d ed., New York: Vintage Books, 1971 (cited: Adversary System).

___: Lon: Anatomy of the Law, New York-Washington-London: Praeger, 1968 (cited: Anatomy).

___: The Forms and Limits of Adjudication, in: 92 Harvard L. Rev. 353-409 (1978), reprinted in: FULLER: The Principles of Social Order, 86-124, Durham: Duke University Press, 1981 (cited: Forms).

___: The Morality of Law, 2d ed., New Haven-London: Yale University Press, 1969 (cited: Morality).

GELLHORN, Ernest: Antitrust Law and Economics in a Nutshell, 2d ed., St. Paul: West Publishing Co., 1981.

GEORGE, Peter: Wesen und Geltungsbereich des Begriffes der Würdigung der

Gesamtwirtschaftlichen Lage und Entwicklung in § 70 IV Satz 2 des GWB, Diss., Frankfurt/M.: 1963.

GERMANN, Oskar Adolf: Grundlagen der Rechtswissenschaft, 2d ed., Bern: Verlag Stämpfli & Cie., 1968 (cited: Grundlagen).

___: Probleme und Methoden der Rechtsfindung, Bern: Verlag Stämpfli & Cie., 1965 (cited: Probleme).

___: Rechtssicherheit, in: Schweizerische Zeitschrift für Strafrecht, vol. 49 (1935), 257-330, reprinted in GERMANN: Methodische Grundfragen, 54-77, Basel: Verlag für Recht und Gesellschaft, 1946 (cited according to reprint: Rechtssicherheit).

GÖHLER, Erich and BUDDENDIEK, Hans: Gesetz über Ordnungswidrigkeiten, 7th ed., München: C. H. Beck'sche Verlagsbuchhandlung, 1984.

GOODHART, Arthur L.: Precedent in English and Continental Law, in: 50 Law Quarterly Rev. 40-65 (1934) (cited: Precedent).

___: The Ratio Decidendi of a Case, in: 22 Modern L. Rev. 117-24 (1959) (cited: Ratio).

GOODNOW, Frank K.: The Principles of the Administrative Law of the United States, New York-London: G. P. Putnam's Sons, 1905.

GRAY, John Chipman: The Nature and Sources of the Law, 2d ed., New York: Macmillan, 1921, reprint, Gloucester/Mass.: Peter Smith, 1972.

GREEN, Leon: The Development of the Doctrine of Stare Decisis and the Extent to Which It Should Be Applied (first published Chicago 1946), in: GREEN: The Litigation Process in Tort Law, 35-58, 2d ed., Indianapolis-New York: Bobbs-Merrill Co., 1977.

GREEN, Mark et al.: The Closed Enterprise System – Ralph Nader's Study Group Report on Antitrust Enforcement, New York: Bantam Books, 1972.

GREENEWALT, Kent: Discretion and Judicial Decision: The Elusive Quest for the Fetters That Bind Judges, in: 75 Columbia L. Rev. 359-99 (1975).

GRIESSHABER, Herbert: Die Beiladung zum Verfahren in Kartellverwaltungssachen, Diss., Heidelberg: 1967.

GRUNSKY, Wolfgang: Grundlagen des verfahrensrechts – Eine vergleichende Darstellung von ZPO, FGG, VwGO, FGO, SGG, 2d ed., Bielefeld: Gieseking Verlag, 1974.

GRÜTZNER, Winfried: Richtiges Verhalten bei Kartellamtsermittlungen im Unternehmen, 2d ed., Heidelberg: Verlagsgesellschaft Recht und Wirtschaft, 1978.

GÜNTHER, Eberhard: Die Auslegung unbestimmter Rechtsbegriffe des GWB, in: Festschrift für Günther Hartmann 123-32, Köln-Berlin-Bonn-München: Carl Heymanns Verlag, 1976 (cited: Auslegung).

___: Entwurf eines deutschen Gesetzes gegen Wettbewerbsbeschränkungen, in: WuW 1951, 17-40 (cited: Entwurf).

HALBEY, Heinrich: Kartellbehörde und richterliche Kontrolle – Zur Auslegung des § 70 Abs. 4 GWB, in: WRP 1968, 349-52.

HALEY, John O.: Antitrust Sanctions and Remedies: A Comparative Study of German and Japanese Law, in: 59 Washington L. Rev., 471-506 (1984).

HALL, Jerome: General Principles of Criminal Law, 2d ed., Indianapolis-New York: Bobbs-Merrill, 1960.

HAMILTON, Walton and TILL, Irene: Antitrust in Action, U.S. Temporary National Economic Committee – Investigation of Concentration of Economic Power – Monograph No. 16 – Senate Committee Print, 76th Congress, 3rd Session, Washington 1940, reprint, New York: Da Capo, 1974.

HANDLER, Milton: Antitrust in Perspective, The Complementary Roles of Rule and Discretion, New York: Columbia University Press, 1957.

HART, H. L. A.: American Jurisprudence Through English Eyes: The Nightmare and the Noble Dream (first published 11 Georgia L. Rev. 969, 1977), in: HART: Essays in Jurisprudence and Philosophy, 23-44, Oxford: Oxford University Press, 1983 (cited: American Jurisprudence).

___: The Concept of Law, Oxford: Oxford University Press, 1961 (cited: Concept).

HAYEK, Friedrich A.: The Counter-Revolution of Science, 2d ed., Indianapolis: Liberty Press, 1979 (cited: Counter-Revolution).

___: The Constitution of Liberty, Chicago: University of Chicago Press, 1960 (cited: Constitution).

HAZARD, Geoffrey C., Jr.: Ethics in the Practice of Law, New Haven-London: Yale University Press, 1978.

HENKEL, Heinrich: Einführung in die Rechtsphilosophie, München-Berlin: C. H. Beck'sche Verlagsbuchhandlung, 1964.

HERMANNS, Ferdinand: Die Ermittlungsbefugnisse der Kartellbehörden, 2d ed.,

Köln: Deutscher Wirtschaftsdienst, 1978.

HERTIN, Paul-Wolfgang: Die Beteiligten an Kartellverfahren und ihre Rechtsstellung, Diss., Münster: 1969.

HINTZE, Gerhard: Aus der Praxis des Kartellsenats beim Kammergericht, insbesondere die Anwendungsmöglichkeit volkswirtschaftlicher Theorien, in: WuW 1970, 571-82.

HIRSCH, Hans: Das Wettbewerbsrecht im Konflikt zwischen wettbewerbspolitischen Zielen und rechtsstaatlichen Grundsätzen, in: Festschrift für Roper, 35-55, Baden-Baden: Nomos Verlagsgesellschaft, 1980.

HOLDSWORTH, William Searles: Case Law, in: 50 Law Quarterly Rev. 180-95 (1934).

HOLMES, Oliver Wendell, Jr.: The Common Law, Boston 1881, reprint, Boston-Toronto: Little, Brown and Co., 1963.

HOLSENDOLPH, Ernest: "U.S. Settles Phone Suit, Drops I.B.M. Case," in: New York *Times*, January 9, 1982, p. 1.

HOPPMANN, Erich: Zum Schutzobjekt des Wettbewerb in: Wettbewerb als Aufgabe, Nach zehn Jahren Gesetz gegen Wettbewerbsbeschränkungen 61-104, Bad Homburg: Verlag Gehlen, 1968.

HUBER, Ernst Rudolf: Wirtschaftsverwaltungsrecht, 2 vols., 2d ed., Tübingen: J. C. B. Mohr, 1953-1954.

IMMENGA, Ulrich and MESTMÄCKER, Ernst-Joachim (ed.): GWB – Gesetz gegen Wettbewerbsbeschränkungen – Kommentar, München: C. H. Beck'sche Verlagsbuchhandlung, 1981.

JAMES, Fleming and HAZARD, Geoffrey C., Jr.: Civil Procedure, 2d ed., Boston-Toronto: Little, Brown and Co., 1977.

JAUERNIG, Othmar: Zivilprozeßrecht, 20th ed., München: C. H. Beck'sche Verlagsbuchhandlung, 1983.

JESCHECK, Hans-Heinrich: Lehrbuch des Strafrechts, Allgemeiner Teil, 3d ed., Berlin: Duncker & Humblot, 1978.

JORDE, Thomas: The Seventh Amendment Right to Jury Trial of Antitrust Issues, in: 69 California L. Rev. 1 (1981).

KADISH, Mortimer R. and KADISH, Sanford H.: Discretion to Disobey, Stanford: Stanford University Press, 1973.

KARLEN, Delmar: Appellate Courts in the United States and England, New York: New York University Press, 1963.

KARTTE, Wolfgang: Wettbewerbspolitik im Spannungsfeld zwischen Bundeswirtschaftsministerium und Bundeskartellamt, in: Festschrift für Eberhard Günther, 47-57, Baden-Baden: Nomos Verlagsgesellschaft, 1976.

KATZMANN, Robert A.: Regulatory Bureaucracy – The Federal Trade Commission, Cambridge/Mass.: M.I.T. Press, 1980.

KAYSEN, Carl: United States v. United Shoe Machinery Corporation – An Economic Analysis of an Anti-Trust Case, Cambridge/Mass.: Harvard University Press, 1956.

KAYSEN, Carl and TURNER, Donald: Antitrust Policy – An Economic and Legal Analysis, Cambridge/Mass.: Harvard University Press, 1959.

KENT, James: Commentaries on American Law, vol. 1, 14th ed., Boston: Little, Brown and Co., 1896.

KIENAST, Peter J.: Consent Settlements im Amerikanischen Antitrust Verfahren, Diessenhofen: Verlag Rüegger, 1978.

KOCH, Eckart: Wirtschaftswissenschaften für Juristen, München: C. H. Beck'sche Verlagsbuchhandlung, 1976.

KOCH, Hans-Joachim: Unbestimmte Rechtsbegriffe und Ermessensermächtigungen im Verwaltungsrecht, Frankfurt/M.: Alfred Metzner Verlag, 1979.

KRAFT, Alfons: Die Berücksichtigung wirtschaftspolitischer und gesellschaftspolitischer Belange im Rahmen des § 1 UWG, in: Festschrift für Bartholomeyczik, 223-39, Berlin: Duncker & Humblot, 1973.

LAMBSDORFF, Otto Graf: 25 Jahre Bundeskartellamt, in: WuW 1983, 351-57 (cited: 25 Jahre).

___: Geleitwort zur 4. Kartellgesetznovelle, in: WuW 1980, 288 (cited: Geleitwort).

LANGEN, Eugen, NIEDERLEITHINGER, Ernst, RITTER, Leonard and SCHMIDT, Ulrich: Kommentar zum Kartellgesetz, 6th ed., Neuwied-Darmstadt: Hermann Luchterhand Verlag, 1982 (cited: 6th ed.).

LANGEN, Eugen, NEIDERLEITHINGER, Ernst and SCHMIDT, Ulrich: Kommentar zum Kartellgesetz, 5th ed., Neuwied-Darmstadt: Hermann Luchterhand Verlag, 1977 (cited: 5th ed.).

LARENZ, Karl: Methodenlehre der Rechtswissenschaft, 5th ed., Berlin-Heidelberg-

New York-Tokyo: Springer-Verlag, 1983.

LEIBHOLZ, Gerhard: Der Zweck im Recht (first published Prague 1937), in: LEIBHOLZ: Strukturprobleme der modernen Demokratie, 282-93, 3d ed., Frankfurt/M.: Athenäum Fischer, 1974.

LETWIN, William: Law and Economic Policy in America, Chicago: University of Chicago Press, 1965.

LEVI, Edward H.: An Introduction to Legal Reasoning, Chicago: University of Chicago Press, 1949.

LIEBERKNECHT, Otfried: Probleme des Verfahrensrechts in Kartellsachen, in: Schwerpunkte des Kartellrechts 1977/78, 65-81, Köln-Berlin-Bonn-München: Carl Heymanns Verlag, 1979.

LLEWELLYN, Karl Nickerson: The Bramble Bush, 2d ed., New York: Oceana Publications, 1951 (cited: Bramble Bush).

___: The Common Law Tradition – Deciding Appeals, Boston-Toronto: Little, Brown and Co., 1960 (cited: Common Law Tradition).

___: Präjudizienrecht und Rechtsprechung in Amerika, Leipzig: Verlag von Theodor Weicher, 1933 (cited: Präjudizienrecht).

___: The Rule of Law in Our Case-Law of Contracts, in: 47 Yale L.J. 1243-71 (1938) (cited: Rule).

MacCORMICK, Neil: Der Rechtsstaat und die rule of law, in: JZ 1984, 65-70.

MAITLAND, Frederick William: The Constitutional History of England, Cambridge/Eng.: Cambridge University Press, 1908 (cited: Constitutional History).

___: Equity also The Forms of Action at Common Law, Two Courses of Lectures, Cambridge/Eng.: Cambridge University Press, 1909 (cited: Forms of Action).

___ (with individual chapters by MONTAGUE, Francis C.): A Sketch of English Legal History, New York-London: G. P. Putnam's Sons, 1915 (cited: Sketch).

MARGOLICH, David: "Antitrust Post Left by Baxter, Legacy Beyond Mere Policies," in: New York *Times*, December 9, 1983, p. D4.

MASSEL, Mark S.: Competition and Monopoly, Washington: The Brookings Institution, 1962.

MAUNZ, Theodor and ZIPPELIUS, Reinhold: Deutsches Staatsrecht, 26th ed.,

München: C. H. Beck'sche Verlagsbuchhandlung, 1985.

MEIER, Gert: Rechtsstaatsprinzip und Handhabung des GWB, in: WuW 1983, 275-83.

MIKSCH, Leonhard: Wettbewerb als Aufgabe, 2d ed., Godesberg: Verlag Helmut Küpper, 1947.

MÖSCHEL, Wernhard: Die Idee der rule of law und das Kartellrecht heute, in: Festgabe für Hayek, vol. 30 of ORDO: Jahrbuch für die Ordnung von Wirtschaft und Gesellschaft, 295-312, Stuttgart: Gustav Fischer Verlag, 1979 (cited: Idee der rule of law).

___: Preiskontrollen über marktbeherrschende Unternehmen, in: JZ 1975, 393-99 (cited: Preiskontrollen).

MÜLLER, Heinz and GRIES, Gerhard: Kommentar zum Gesetz gegen Wettbewerbsbeschränkungen (Kartellgesetz), Frankfurt/M.: Verlag für Wirtschaftspraxis, 1958.

Note, Flexibility and Finality in Antitrust Consent Decrees, in: 80 Harvard L. Rev. 1303 (1967).

OLIPHANT, Herman: A Return to Stare Decisis, in: 14 A.B.A.J. 71, reprinted in: CHRISTIE, George (ed.): Jurisprudence, 665-82, St. Paul: West Publishing Co., 1973 (cited according to reprint).

OPPENHEIM, S. Chesterfield: Federal Antitrust Legislation: Guideposts to a Revised National Antitrust Policy, in: 50 Michigan L. Rev. 1139-1244 (1952).

OTT, Edward E.: Die Methode der Rechtsanwendung, Zürich: Schulthess Polygraphischer Verlag, 1979.

PFEIFFER, Gerd: Grundfragen der Rechtskontrolle im Kartellverfahren (Auslegungsmethodik – unbestimmte Rechtsbegriffe – Verfahrensrecht), in: Schwerpunkte des Kartellrechts 1978/79, 1-12, Köln-Berlin-Bonn-München: Carl Heymanns Verlag, 1980.

PICKER, Edward: Richterrecht und Richterrechtsetzung, in: JZ 1984, 153-63.

PITOFSKY, Robert: The Political Content of Antitrust, in: 127 U. Pennsylvania L. Rev. 1051-75 (1979).

PLUCKNETT, Theodore F. T.: A Concise History of the Common Law, 5th ed., Boston: Little, Brown and Co., 1956.

POSNER, Richard A.: Antitrust Law – An Economic Perspective, Chicago-London:

University of Chicago Press, 1976.

POUND, Roscoe: Administrative Law, Pittsburgh: University of Pittsburgh Press, 1942 (cited: Administrative Law).

___: Appellate Procedure in Civil Cases, Boston: Little, Brown and Co., 1941 (cited: Appellate Procedure).

___: Justice According to Law, New Haven: Yale University Press, 1951 (cited: Justice).

___: The Theory of Judicial Decision, in: 36 Harvard L. Rev. 641-62, 802-25, 940-59 (1923) (cited: Theory).

RADBRUCH, Gustav: Gesetzliches Unrecht und übergesetzliches Recht, in: Süddeutsche Juristenzeitung (1946) 105-08, reprinted in: RADBRUCH: Rechtsphilosophie 339-50, and in: RADBRUCH: Mensch 111-24 (cited: Gesetzliches Unrecht).

___: Der Mensch im Recht, 3d ed., Göttingen: Vandenhoeck & Ruprecht, 1957 (cited: Mensch).

___: Rechtsphilosophie, 8th ed., Stuttgart: K. F. Koehler Verlag, 1973 (cited: Rechtsphilosophic).

___: Vorschule der Rechtsphilosophie, 3d ed., Göttingen: Vandenhoeck & Ruprecht, 1965 (cited: Vorschule).

RAISER, Thomas: Ökonomen im Bundeskartellamt und in den Kartellgerichten, in: BB 1972, 471-75.

RAWLS, John: A Theory of Justice, Cambridge/Mass.: Harvard University Press, 1972.

RAZ, Joseph: The Rule of Law and Its Virtue: in CUNNINGHAM, L. (ed.): Liberty and the Rule of Law, 3-21, College Station/Texas: Texas A&M University Press, 1979, reprinted in: RAZ: The Authority of Law, 210-29, Oxford: Oxford University Press, 1979.

RESNIK, J.: Managerial Judges, in: 96 Harvard L. Rev. 376 (1982).

RHEINSTEIN, Max: Comparative Law and Legal Systems, in: International Encyclopedia of the Social Sciences, vol. 9, 204-10, New York: Macmillan, 1968.

RINCK, Gerd: Wirtschaftsrecht, 4th ed., Köln-Berlin-München-Bonn: Carl Heymanns Verlag, 1974.

RITTNER, Fritz: Einführung in das Wettbewerbs- und Kartellrecht, Heidelberg-Karlsruhe: C. F. Müller Juristischer Verlag, 1981 (cited: Einführung).

___: Das Ermessen der Kartellbehörde, in: Festschrift für Heinz Kaufmann, 307-25, Köln: Verlag Dr. Otto Schmidt, 1972 (cited: Ermessen).

___: § 22 GWB im Spannungsfeld wirtschaftswissenschaftlicher Theorien und rechtsstaatlicher Postulate, Festschrift für Günther Hartmann, Köln: Carl Heymanns Verlag, 1976 (cited: Spannungsfeld).

___: Die Rechtssicherheit im Kartellrecht, in: WuW 1969, 63-81 (cited: Rechtssicherheit).

ROBERT, Rüdiger: Konzentrationspolitik in der Bundesrepublik – Das Beispiel der Entstehung des Gesetzes gegen Wettbewerbsbeschränkungen, Berlin: Duncker & Humblot, 1976.

ROSENBERG, Leo and SCHWAB, Karl Heinz: Zivilprozeßrecht, 13th ed., München: C. H. Beck'sche Verlagsbuchhandlung, 1981.

RÜMELIN, Max: Die Rechtssicherheit, Tübingen: J. C. B. Mohr, 1924.

RÜTHERS, Bernd: Die unbegrenzte Auslegung – Zum Wandel der Privatrechtsordnung im Nationalsozialismus, 2d ed., Kronberg/Ts.: Athenäum Fischer, 1973.

SALINGER, H. D.: Das Gesetz zur Schaffung der Diktatur eines Bundeskartellamtes, Düsseldorf: Walter Rau Verlag, (n.d. [1952]).

SALTZBURG, Stephen A.: The Unnecessarily Expanding Role of the American Trial Judge, in: 64 Virginia L. Rev. 1-81 (1978).

SATTELMACHER, Paul and SIRP, Wilhelm: Bericht, Gutachten und Urteil, 29th ed., München: Verlag Franz Vahlen, 1983.

SCHERER, F. M.: Industrial Market Structure and Economic Performance, 2d ed., Boston: Rand McNally College Publishing, 1980.

SCHLESINGER, Rudolf B.: Comparative Criminal Procedure: A Plea for Utilizing Foreign Experience, in: 26 Buffalo L. Rev. 361-85 (1977).

SCHMIDT, Eberhard: Lehrkommentar zur Strafprozeßordnung und zum Gerichtsverfassungsgesetz, Teil 1, 2d ed., Göttingen: Vandenhoeck & Ruprecht, 1964 (cited: Lehrkommentar).

SCHMIDT, Karsten: Kartellverfahrensrecht – Kartellverwaltungsrecht – Bürgerliches Recht, Köln-Berlin-Bonn-München: Carl Heymanns Verlag, 1977 (cited: Kartellverfahrensrecht).

___: Der Zivilrichter als "Schöpfer" und "Vollstrecker" wirtschaftsrechtlicher Normen, in: DRiZ 1977, 97-102 (cited: Zivilrichter).

SCHMIDT-BLEIBTREU, Bruno and KLEIN, Franz: Kommentar zum Grundgesetz, 5th ed., Neuwied-Darmstadt: Hermann Luchterhand Verlag, 1980.

SCHNEIDER, Werner H. A.: Aufgaben, Organisation und Bisherige Praxis des Deutschen Bundeskartellamtes, Diss., Bern: 1966.

SCHOLZ, Franz: Die Rechtssicherheit, Berlin: Walter de Gruyter & Co., 1955.

SCHUMANN, Karl F.: Der Handel mit Gerechtigkeit, Frankfurt/M.: Suhrkamp Verlag, 1977.

SCHWARTZ, Bernard: Administrative Law, Boston-Toronto: Little, Brown and Co., 1976.

SEIDENFUS, ST., Helmuth and EWERS, Hans-Jürgen: Wettbewerbspolitik und die Aufgabe der Gerichte, in: Festschrift für G. Hartmann, 303-36, Köln-Berlin-Bonn-München: Carl Heymanns Verlag, 1976.

SHENEFIELD, John H.: Statement before the Committee on the Judiciary, United States House of Representatives, in: Commerce Clearing House, Inc. (CCH): Trade Regulation Reports, No. 326, Part II, March 27, 1978.

SHIPMAN, Benjamin J.: Handbook of Common-Law Pleading, 3d ed., St. Paul: West Publishing Co., 1923.

SMITH, William F., Attorney General: Speech from June 24, 1981, reprinted in: Commerce Clearing House Trade Regulation Reports, § 50,430 (June 29, 1981).

SOELL, Hermann: Das Ermessen der Eingriffsverwaltung, Heidelberg: Carl Winter Universitätsverlag, 1973.

SPENGLER, Albrecht: Über die Tatbestandsmäßigkeit und Rechtswidrigkeit von Wettbewerbsbeschränkungen, in: WuW Schriftenreihe Issue 6, 23-46, Düsseldorf: Verlag Handelsblatt, 1960.

SPERLICH, Peter: The case for preserving trial by jury in complex civil litigation, in: 65 Judicature 394-419 (1982).

SPRECHER, Robert A.: The Development of the Doctrine of Stare Decisis and the Extent to Which It Should Be Applied, in: 31 A.B.A.J. 501 (1945), reprinted in: FRYER, William T. and BENSON, Corville D.: Cases and Materials on Legal Method, 718-38, St. Paul: West Publishing Co., 1949 (cited according to reprint).

STEINDORFF, Ernst: Einführung in das Wirtschaftsrecht der Bundesrepublik

Deutschland, Darmstadt: Wissenschaftliche Buchgesellschaft, 1977 (cited: Einführung).

___: Gesetzgeberische Möglichkeiten zu verbesserter Durchsetzung des Gesetzes gegen Wettbewerbsbeschränkungen, in: ZHR 1974, 504-32 (cited: Möglichkeiten).

___: Politik des Gesetzes als Auslegungsmaßstab im Wirtschaftsrecht, in: Festschrift für Karl Larenz, 217-44, München: C. H. Beck'sche Verlagsbuchhandlung, 1973 (cited: Politik des Gesetzes).

___: Zweckmäßigkeit im Wettbewerbsrecht, Frankfurt/M.: Vittorio Klostermann, 1959 (cited: Zweckmäßigkeit).

STELKENS, Paul, BONK, Heinz and LEONHARDT, Klaus: Verwaltungsverfahrensgesetz, Kommentar, München: C. H. Beck'sche Verlagsbuchhandlung, 1978.

STEPHEN, James F.: A General View of the Criminal Law of England, London-Cambridge/Eng.: Macmillan & Co., 1863, reprint, Littleton/Col.: Fred B. Rothman & Co., 1985.

STONE, Julius: The Ratio of the Ratio Decidendi, in: 22 Modern L. Rev. 597-620 (1959).

SULLIVAN, Lawrence Anthony: Handbook of the Law of Antitrust, St. Paul: West Publishing Co., 1977.

SUMMERS, Robert S.: Instrumentalism and American Legal Theory, Ithaca-London: Cornell University Press, 1982 (cited: Instrumentalism).

___: Professor Fuller on Morality and Law, (first published St. Paul 1966), in: More Essays in Legal Philosophy, 101-30, Berkeley-Los Angeles: University of California Press, 1971 (cited: Professor Fuller).

THAL, Steven Henry: Die Geltung einer Rule of Reason im deutschen Kartellrecht, in: WuW 1970, 319-25.

THIEME, Werner: Verwaltungslehre, 3d ed., Köln-Berlin-Bonn-München: Carl Heymanns Verlag, 1977.

THOMPSON, Seymour D.: A Treatise on the Law of Trials, 2 vols., Chicago: T. H. Flood & Co., 1889.

THUROW, Lester C.: The Zero Sum Society, New York: Basic Books, 1980.

TOMLINSON, Edward A.: Nonadversarial Justice: The French Experience, in: 42 Maryland L. Rev. 131-95 (1983).

ULE, Carl Hermann: Verwaltungsgerichtsbarkeit, Kommentar, 2d ed., Köln-Berlin-Bonn-München: Carl Heymanns Verlag, 1962 (cited: Verwaltungsgerichtsbarkeit).

___: Verwaltungsprozeßrecht, 8th ed., München: C. H. Beck'sche Verlagsbuchhandlung, 1983 (cited: Verwaltungsprozeßrecht).

___: Zur Anwendung unbestimmter Rechtsbegriffe im Verwaltungsrecht, in: BACHOF, Otto (ed.), Forschungen und Berichte aus dem öffentlichen Recht; Gedächtnisschrift für Walter Jellinek, 309-30, München: Isar Verlag, 1955 (cited: ULE, Anwendung).

VELTINS, Michael Alexander and VELTINS, Jutta: Zuläßigkeit und Grenzen der Mehrerlösabschöpfung nach § 37b GWB, in: WRP 1981, 619-23.

WASSERSTROM, Richard A.: The Judicial Decision, Stanford: Stanford University Press, 1971.

WEAVER, Suzanne: Decision to Prosecute: Organization and Public Policy in the Antitrust Division, Cambridge/Mass.: The M.I.T. Press, 1977.

WEBER, Max: Wirtschaft und Gesellschaft, 4th ed., 2 vols., Tübingen: J. C. B. Mohr, 1956, English trans.: Economy and Society, Berkeley-Los Angeles-London: University of California Press, 1968.

WEIDES, Peter: Verwaltungsverfahren und Widerspruchsverfahren, 2d ed., München: C. H. Beck'sche Verlagsbuchhandlung, 1981.

WEIGEND, Thomas: Anklagepflicht und Ermessen, Baden-Baden: Nomos Verlagsgesellschaft, 1978.

WESSEL, Milton R.: The Rule of Reason: A New Approach to Corporate Litigation, Reading/Mass.: Addison-Wesley Publishing Co., 1976.

WESTRICK, K. and LÖWENHEIM, U.: Gesetz gegen Wettbewerbsbeschränkungen, Herne: Verlag Neue Wirtschafts-Briefe, 1979.

WHITE, Peter: F.T.C.: Wrong Agency for the Job of Adjudication, in: 61 A.B.A.J. 1242-45 (1975).

WIECKMANN, Hans-Joachim: Das Auskunftsersuchen im System kartellbehördlicher Eingriffsbefugnisse, Frankfurt/M.: Peter Lang, 1977.

WIEDEMANN, Herbert: Rechtssicherheit – Ein Absoluter Wert?, in: Festschrift für Karl Larenz, 199-215, München: C. H. Beck'sche Verlagsbuchhandlung, 1973.

WINFIELD, Percy H.: Public Policy in the English Common Law, in: 42 Harvard L. Rev. 76-102 (1928).

WITHROW, James R. and LARMS, Richard P.: The "Big" Antitrust Case: 25 Years of Sisyphean Labor, in: 62 Cornell L. Rev. 1-49 (1976).

WOLFF, Hans J. and BACHOF, Otto: Verwaltungsrecht, vol. 1, 9th ed., München: C. H. Beck'sche Verlagsbuchhandlung, 1974.

WÜRDINGER, Hans: Rechtskontrolle der Verfügungen der Kartellbehörden durch die Gerichte (§ 70 Abs. 4 GWB), Karlsruhe: C. F. Müller Verlag, 1958, also in: WuW 1958, 392-407.

WYZANSKI, Charles E. Jr.: Whereas – A Judge's Premises, Boston: Little, Brown and Co., 1965.

ZUCK, Rüdiger: Bundeskartellamt, Dienstaufsicht und Regress, in: NJW 1972, 468-72 (cited: Dienstaufsicht).

___: Bundeskartellamt und Bundeswirtschaftsministerium, in: BB 1973, 20-23 (cited: Bundeswirtschaftsministerium).

___: Bundeskartellamt und Wirtschaftspolitik, in: NJW 1971, 1633-36 (cited: Wirtschaftspolitik).

Abbreviations of Sources

A.B.A.J.	American Bar Association Journal.
A.B.A. F.T.C. Report	American Bar Association: Report of the ABA Commission to Study the Federal Trade Commission, Chicago 1969.
A.B.A. Model Code	___: Model Code of Professional Responsibility, Chicago 1981, reprinted in: Martindale-Hubbel Law Directory, Vol. 7, Summit/N.J. 1983.
A.B.A Model Rules	___: Model Rules of Professional Conduct, Chicago 1983, reprinted in: Martindale-Hubbel Law Directory, Vol. 7, Summit/N.J. 1984.
A.B.A. Rule of Law	___: Section on International and Comparative Law: The Rule of Law in the United States, A Statement by the Committee to Cooperate with the International Commission of Jurists, Hague 1958.
ALR	Allgemeines Landrecht für die Preußischen Staaten of June 1, 1794, cited following HATTENHAUER, Hans and BUSCHMANN, Arno: Textbuch zur Privatrechtsgeschichte der Neuzeit, § 95, München: C. H. Beck'sche Verlagsbuchhandlung, 1967.
Antitrust Enforcement	United States Department of Justice: Antitrust Enforcement – The Antitrust Division: How It works; Enforcement Plans, published in: Commerce Clearing House (CCH) Trade Regulation Reports, No. 326, Part II, March 27, 1978.
Antitrust L.J.	Antitrust Law Journal.

Att'y Gen. Nat'l Committee	Attorney General's National Committee to Study the Antitrust Laws: Report, Washington 1955.
BAnz	Bundesanzeiger (government periodical).
Bay Kartellbericht 1979	Bayerisches Staatsministerium für Wirtschaft und Verkehr als Landeskartellbehörde: Kartellbericht 1978/1979, München 1980.
BB	Betriebsberater (periodical).
BegrGWB	Begründung zu dem Entwurf eines Gesetzes gegen Wettbewerbsbeschränkungen, Supplement 1 to Bundestagsdrucksache II/1158, pp. 21 ff., reprinted in: WuW 1952, 460 ff.
BGB	Bürgerliches Gesetzbuch (Civil Code) of January 18, 1896.
BGHZ	Entscheidungen des Bundesgerichtshofs in Zivilsachen.
Buffalo L. Rev.	Buffalo Law Review.
BVerfGE	Entscheidungen des Bundesverfassungsgerichts.
California L. Rev.	California Law Review.
BVwGE	Entscheidungen des Bundesverwaltungsgerichts.
Clayton Act	38 Stat. 730 ff., as amended = 15 U.S.C. §§ 12 to 27.
Cornell L. Rev.	Cornell Law Review.
DRiZ	Deutsche Richterzeitung (periodical).
Eng. Rep.	English Reports – Full Reprint, Edinburgh-London 1900-1932.

F.2d	West Publishing Co.: Federal Reporter – Second Series.
Fed. R. Civ. P.	Federal Rules of Civil Procedure.
Fed. R. Crim. P.	Federal Rules of Criminal Procedure.
F. Supp.	West Publishing Co.: Federal Supplement.
F.T.C. Act	38 Stat. 717 ff., as amended = 15 U.S.C. §§ 41 to 51.
GG	Grundgesetz (constitution) of May 23, 1949.
GRUR	Gewerblicher Rechtsschutz und Urheberrecht (periodical).
GWB	Gesetz gegen Wettbewerbsbeschränkungen (Law Against Trade Restraints) in the version from September 24, 1980.
Harvard L. Rev.	Harvard Law Review.
H. Rep. No. 96-874 874	United States Congress, House of Representatives, 96th Congress, 2d Sess., Report No. 96- Judiciary Committee from April 14, 1980, reprinted in 1980 United States Code Congressional and Administrative News 2752 ff.
Judicature	Judicature.
JZ	Juristenzeitung (periodical).
L. Ed. 2d	Lawyers Cooperative Publishing Co. and Bancroft-Whitney Publishing Co.: United States Supreme Court Reports, Lawyers' Edition, 2d series.
Law Quarterly Rev.	Law Quarterly Review.

Maryland L. Rev.	Maryland Law Review.
Merger Guidelines (1984)	United States Department of Justice, Merger Guidelines of June 14, 1984, reprinted in: Commerce Clearing House, Inc., Trade Regulation Reporter, 12th ed. (loose leaf), Vol. 2, ¶¶4490-95.
Merger Guidelines (1982)	United States Department of Justice, Merger Guidelines, Explanation and Summary of June 14, 1982, reprinted in: Commerce Clearing House, Inc., Trade Regulation Reporter, 12th ed. (loose leaf), ¶¶4500-05.
Merger Guidelines (1968)	United States Department of Justice, Merger Guidelines of June 30, 1968, reprinted in: Commerce Clearing House, Inc., Trade Regulation Reporter, 12th ed. (loose leaf), ¶4510.
Michigan L. Rev.	Michigan Law Review.
MRG Nr. 56	Militärregierungsgesetz Nr. 56 of Feb. 12, 1947, Amtsblatt der amerikanischen Militärregierung of April 1, 1947, 2 ff.
Modern L. Rev.	Modern Law Review.
National Commission	National Commission for the Review of Antitrust Laws and Procedures: Report to the President and the Attorney General, 2 Vols., Washington, 1979.
National Commission Staff Paper (with title)	National Commission for the Review of Antitrust Law and Procedures, reports prepared by the staff of the commission in 1978 for it (not adopted by the commission) in: 48 Antitrust L.J. 1017-1327 (1980) (cited with the title of the report).
NJW	Neue Juristische Wochenschrift (periodical).

N.Y.S.2d	West Publishing Co.: New York Supplement – Second Series.
OWiG	Gesetz über Ordnungswidrigkeiten (Law on Regulatory Infractions) in the version of January 2, 1975.
PotsdAbk	Potsdam Agreement of August 12, 1945.
Prettyman Report	Judicial Conference of the United States: Procedure in Anti-Trust and other Protracted Cases, Washington 1951, reprinted in: 8 F.R.D. 62 ff.
Pub. L. 93-528	88 Stat. 1706 ff.; § 2 = 15 U.S.C. 16 (b) to (h).
Pub. L. 96-349	94 Stat. 1157 ff., § 5(a) = 15 U.S.C. § 16(a).
S. Ct.	West Publishing Co.: Supreme Court Reporter.
Sherman Act	26 Stat. 209, as amended = 15 U.S.C. §§ 1 to 7.
Stat.	United States Statutes at Large.
TB 1983/1984	Bericht des Bundeskartellamtes über seine Tätigkeit in den Jahren 1983/1984 sowie über die Lage und Entwicklung auf seinem Aufgabengebiet (§ 50 GWB), Bundestag Drucksache 10/3550 Bonn 1985.
TB 1981/1982	Bericht . . . in den Jahren 1981/1982 . . . , Bundestag Drucksache 10/243, Bonn 1983.
TB 1979/1980	Bericht . . . in den Jahren 1979/1980 . . . , Bundestag Drucksache 9/565, Bonn 1981.
Trade Cases	Commerce Clearing House, Inc. (CCH): Trade Cases.

U. Pennsylvania L. Rev.	University of Pennsylvania Law Review.
U.S.	United States Reports.
U.S.C.	United States Code.
U.S. Const.	United States Constitution of September 17, 1787 as amended.
UWG	Gesetz gegen unlauteren Wettbewerb (Law Against Unfair Competition) of June 7, 1909.
Virginia L. Rev.	Virginia Law Review.
Vorläufiger Bericht	Vorläufiger Bericht der deutschen Kommission zum Studium von Kartell- und Monopolfragen in den Vereinigten Staaten, published as a supplement to Bundesanzeiger No. 250 of December 29, 1950.
VwGO	Verwaltungsgerichtsordnung (Law Governing Administrative Courts) of January 21, 1960.
VwVfG	Verwaltungsverfahrensgesetz (Administrative Procedure Law) of May 25, 1970.
Washington L. Rev.	Washington Law Review.
WRP	Wirtschaft in Recht und Praxis (periodical).
WuW	Wirtschaft und Wettbewerb (periodical).
WuW/E	Wirtschaft und Wettbewerb/Entscheidung Sammlung.
Yale L.J.	Yale Law Journal.
ZfRV	Zeitschrift für Rechtsvergleichung (periodical).

ZHR — Zeitschrift für das gesamte Handelsrecht (periodical).

ZPO — Zivilprozeßordnung (Civil Procedure Code) in the version of September 12, 1950.

Table of Cases

DECISIONS OF GERMAN COURTS

Bundesgerichtshof (Federal Supreme Court)

BGHZ 68, 6 = WuW 1977, 338 = WuW/E BGH 1458 ("Fertigbeton")
WuW 1980, 819 = WuW/E BGH 1717 ("Haus und Hofkanalguß")
WuW 1981, 346 = WuW/E BGH 1758 ("Schleifscheiben und Schleifkörper")
WuW 1981, 541 = WuW/E BGH 1787 ("Garant")

Bundesverfassungsgericht (Federal Constitutional Court)

BVerfGE 3, 327
BVerfGE 49, 168

Bundesverwaltungsgericht (Federal Supreme Administrative Court)

BVwGE 8, 350 = GRUR 1959, 435 ("Patentamt")

DECISIONS OF COMMON LAW COURTS

Associated General Contractors v. *California State Carpenters Council*, 459 U.S. 519 (1983).
Becker v. *Interstate Properties*, 569 F.2d 1203. (3d Cir. 1977).
Bernhardt v. *Polygraphic Co. of America*, 350 U.S. 198 (1955).
Blanton v. *Mobil Oil Corp.*, 721 F.2d 1207 (9th Cir. 1983).
Blonder-Tongue Laboratories, Inc. v. *University of Illinois Foundation*, 402 U.S. 313 (1971).
Bose Corp. v. *Consumers Union*, 466 U.S. 485 (1984).
Brady v. *Maryland*, 373 U.S. 83 (1963).
Broadcast Music, Inc. v. *Columbia Broadcasting System, Inc.* 441 U.S. 1 (1979).
Brown Shoe Co. v. *United States*, 370 U.S. 294 (1962).
Brunswick Corp. v. *Pueblo Bowl-O-Mat, Inc.*, 429 U.S. 477 (1977).

Bushell's Case, Vaughn 135, 124 Eng. Rep. 1006 (Common Pleas 1670).

Cantor v. *Detroit Edison*, 428 U.S. 579 (1976).

Chicago Board of Trade v. *United States*, 246 U.S. 231 (1918).

Cicio v. *City of New York*, 98 A.D.2d 38, 469 N.Y.S.2d 467 (1983).

City of Lafayette v. *Louisiana Power & Light Co.*, 435 U.S. 389 (1978).

Continental T.V. Inc. v. *GTE Sylvania, Inc.*, 433 U.S. 36 (1977).

Cooper v. *American Airlines*, 149 F.2d 355 (2d Cir. 1945).

Flood v. *Kuhn*, 443 F.2d 264 (2d Cir. 1971), *aff'd* 407 U.S. 258, (1972).

Ford Motor Co. v. *United States (Autolite)*, 405 U.S. 562 (1979).

Fruehauf Corp. v. *FTC*, 603 F.2d 345 (2d Cir. 1979).

Galloway v. *United States*, 319 U.S. 372 (1943).

Graphic Products Distributors, Inc. v. *ITEK Corp.*, 717 F.2d 1560 (11th Cir. 1983).

Hartford-Empire Co. v. *United States*, 323 U.S. 386 (1945).

Hasbrouck v. *Texaco, Inc.*, 663 F.2d 930 (9th Cir. 1981).

Hertz v. *Woodman*, 218 U.S. 205 (1910).

ILC Peripherals Leasing Corp. (Memorex) v. *IBM Corp.*, 458 F. Supp. 428, (N. D. Cal. 1977), *aff'd* 636 F.2d 1188 (9th Cir. 1980).

Illinois Brick Co. v. *Illinois*, 431 U.S. 720 (1977).

Jefferson Parish Hospital District No. 2 v. *Hyde*, 466 U.S. 2 (1984).

Jones v. *Barnes*, 463 U.S. 745 (1983).

J. Truett Payne Co. v. *Chrysler Motors Corp.*, 451 U.S. 557 (1981).

Klor's Inc. v. *Broadway – Hale Stores, Inc.*, 359 U.S. 207 (1959).

Marrese v. *American Academy of Orthopedic Surgeons* 629 F.2d 1083 (7th Cir. 1982), *vacated en banc, id. again decided* (1983), 706 F.2d 1488 (7th Cir. 1983), *again vacated en banc id., decided en banc* 726 F.2d 1150 (7th Cir. 1984), *reversed* ___ U.S. ___, 105 S.Ct. 1327, 84 L. Ed. 2d 274 (1985).

McLain v. *Real Estate Board of New Orleans, Inc.*, 444 U.S. 232 (1980).

Mitchell v. *Reynolds*, 1 Peere Williams 181, 24 Eng. Rep. 347 (Queen's Bench 1711).

Monsanto Co. v. *Spray Rite Service Corp.*, 465 U.S. 752 (1984).

Myers v. *Bethlehem Shipbuilding Corp.*, 303 U.S. 41 (1938).

National Society of Professional Engineers v. *United States*, 435 U.S. 679 (1978).

Nevada v. *United States*, 464 U.S. 154 (1983).

Northern Pacific Railway Co. v. *United States*, 356 U.S. 1 (1958).

Northwest Power Products, Inc. v. *Omark Industries, Inc.*, 578 F.2d 83 (5th Cir. 1978).
Overseas Motors, Inc. v. *Import Motors, Ltd.*, 375 F. Supp. 499 (E. D. Mich. 1974), *aff'd* 519 F.2d 119 (6th Cir. 1975).
Parker v. *Brown*, 317 U.S. 341 (1943).
Parklane Hosiery Co. v. *Shore*, 439 U.S. 322 (1979).
Pullman-Standard Division v. *Swint*, 456 U.S. 273 (1982).
Schwegmann Bros., Inc. v. *Calvert Distillers Corp.*, 341 U.S. 384 (1951).
SCM Corp. v. *Xerox Corp.*, 463 F. Supp. 982 (D. Conn. 1978).
Sears, Roebuck & Co. v. *Stiffel Co.*, 376 U.S. 225 (1964).
Smith v. *Allwright*, 321 U.S. 649 (1944).
Southern Pacific Co. v. *Jensen*, 244 U.S. 205 (1917).
Spector Motor Service v. *Walsh*, 139 F.2d 809 (2d Cir. 1944).
Standard Oil Co. of New Jersey v. *United States*, 221 U.S. 1 (1911).
Swift & Co. v. *United States*, 265 U.S. 311 (1928).
United States v. *Aluminum Co. of America*, 148 F.2d 416 (2d Cir. 1945).
United States v. *American Cyanamid Co.*, 719 F.2d 558 (2d Cir. 1983).
United States v. *Arnold, Schwinn & Co.*, 388 U.S. 365 (1967).
United States v. *Bechtel Corp.*, 648 F.2d 660 (9th Cir. 1981).
United States v. *Grinnell Corp.*, 384 U.S. 563 (1966).
United States v. *Mendoza*, 464 U.S. 154 (1984).
United States v. *Parke Davis & Co.*, 362 U.S. 29 (1960).
United States v. *Socony-Vacuum Oil Co.*, 310 U.S. 150 (1940).
United States v. *Swift & Co.*, 286 U.S. 106 (1932).
United States v. *Swift & Co.*, 189 F. Supp 885 (N. D. Ill. 1960), *aff'd* 367 U.S. 909 (1961).
United States v. *Topco Associates*, 405 U.S. 596 (1972).
Zenith Radio Corp. v. *Matsushita Elec. Indus. Co.*, 478 F.Supp. 889 (E.D. 1979), *vacated* 631 F.2d 1069 (3d Cir. 1980).

Notes

INTRODUCTION

The notes utilize a short form citation; full bibliographic information is contained in the bibliography. Citation style of periodical articles and court decisions follows American legal style for American materials and German style for German materials. Thus 62 Cornell L. Rev. 768 (1977) refers to volume 62, page 768; similarly, WuW 1981, 20 refers to volume 1981, page 20.

Citations to German statutes follow the usual German style. An abbreviation gives the name of the law (for example, BGB, GWB, VwVfG) and a section sign and Arabic numeral, the section of the law. A following Roman numeral gives the paragraph of the particular section (even where the original law uses Arabic numerals to designate paragraphs). An additional Arabic numeral following the Roman numeral, without further designation, gives the sentence of the paragraph. Thus § 41 I 1 VwVfG refers to section 41, paragraph 1, sentence 1 of the Administrative Procedure Law.

Citations to sections without designation of a particular law are to the GWB.

The GWB and other German laws cited are printed in many different convenient private editions, with and without commentary. A convenient single volume text edition containing the laws in force cited, except the VwVfG and VwGO, is Schönfelder, Deutsche Gesetze (63d ed. 1985), which is regularly updated. Sartorius, Deutsche Verfassungs- und Verwaltungsgesetze, volume 1 (1984) is a convenient single volume containing the VwVfG and VwGO (as well as the GG).

Translations are the author's unless otherwise indicated. English translations of the complete GWB as currently in force include: R. Mueller, M. Heidenhain and H. Schneider, *German Antitrust Law,* 3d ed., Frankfurt/M.: Fritz Knapp Verlag, 1984; M. Riesenkampf and J. Gres, Law Against Restraints of Competition with 1980 Amendments, Köln: Verlag Dr. Otto Schmidt, 1980; F. Beier, G. Schricker and W. Fikentscher, German Industrial Property, Copyright and Antitrust Laws, Weinheim: Verlag Chemie, 1983.

CHAPTER 1

1. For example, No. 12 PotsAbk; introduction to MRG No. 56; ARNOLD, BOTTLENECKS 15 ff.; BORKIN/WELSH; i ff.

2. See generally MRG N. 56; BAUMBACH/HEFERMEHL, 7th ed., 622 ff.; HUBER, Vol. 1, 335 ff.

3. Art. 1 of the Second Part of ZusatzAbk zu Generalvertrag in: WuW 1952, 63.

4. LAMBSDORFF, WuW 1983, 351.

5. BARBIER 4.

6. "Antitrust Grows Unpopular," in: Business Week, intern. ed. from Jan. 12, 1981, 63. See BORK, Paradox; THUROW 145 ff.

7. MARGOLICH 4.

8. See FIKENTSCHER, Methoden, Vol. 1, 13 ff.

9. See, for example, BOK, 74 Harvard L. Rev. 226; KAYSEN/TURNER, Ch. 8; LETWIN 279 ff.; OPPENHEIM, 50 Michigan L. Rev. 1139, 1145 ff.

10. See BORK, Paradox, Ch. 22.

11. See FIKENTSCHER, Theorie 162 f.

12. For German law, see FORSTHOFF 5 ff.; GRUNSKY 1 ff.; von MÜNCH, in: ERICHSEN/MARTENS § 1; WOLFF/BACHOF, Vol. 1, §§ 20 f.; BVwGE 8, 350 (*Patentamt*); for American law, see, DAVIS, Administrative Law, Ch. 1; FULLER, Forms, 72 Harvard L. Rev. 353; GOODNOW, Ch. 1; POUND, Administrative Law 4 ff.; POUND, Justice, Part 3; SCHWARTZ §§ 4, 10.

13. See, for example, GRAY, 1: "The Law of a community consists of the general rules which are followed by its judicial department in establishing legal rights and duties." GRAY 1. Compare *Associated General Contractors* v. *California State Carpenters Council*, 459 U.S. 519, 532. For the beginnings of the Sherman Act, see LETWIN.

14. MYERS' principal work was Deutsches Verwaltungsrecht, 3d ed., 1924.

15. See RITTNER, Spannungsfeld 259 f.

16. The leading representatives of this school and their principal works were: BÖHM, Franz: Wettbewerb und Monopolkampf (1933); EUCKEN, Walter: Die Grundlagen der Nationalökonomie (1st ed., 1940) and Die Grundsätze der Wirtschaftspolitik (1st ed., 1952); MIKSCH, Leonard: Wettbewerb als Aufgabe (1st ed., 1937). Compare Fikentscher, Wirtschaftsrecht 41 ff. Böhm, as a member of the Bundestag, headed the government commission which visited the United States to study American antitrust law. See VORLÄUFIGER BERICHT. For the beginnings of the GWB, see FIKENTSCHER, Entwicklung; FIKENTSCHER, Kartellrechtswissenschaft, WuW 1955, 201; GÜNTHER, Entwurf, WuW 1951, 17. See also ROBERT; SALINGER.

17. See, for example, HOPPMANN 85. Because this viewpoint was adopted in the GWB, see the text accompanying note 19 below, the criticism of American antitrust law made by Robert Bork applies to German cartel law as well. According to Bork, the present crisis in American antitrust results because American antitrust law pursues noneconomic policy goals, while it should be limited to improving consumer welfare. See BORK, Paradox 7, 405. Since this criticism applies to both German and American antitrust law, it does not explain why the antitrust laws are so differently judged in the two countries.

18. See EUCKEN, Grundsätze 53 ff.; MIKSCH 10 ff.

19. For explicit example, see BegrGWB Part A, I; GÜNTHER, Entwurf, WuW 1951, 17, 22. See EUCKEN, Grundsätze 175 ff.; MIKSCH 214 ff.

20. BegrGWB Part A, III (translation from WuW 1952, 450).

21. GÜNTHER, Entwurf, WuW 1951, 17, 22; MIKSCH 220 ff. This neoliberal principle adopts the slogan: "Competition as mission" (*Wettbewerb als Aufgabe*), BÄHR et al. 5 ff.; MIKSCH, title page. See also STEINDORFF, Einführung 15.

22. See RINCK 1. Also see STEINDORFF, Einführung 7.

23. See EUCKEN, Grundsätze 48 ff.; HIRSCH 35 f.

24. See BÄHR et al. 12.

25. See note 21 above.

CHAPTER 2

26. See MacCORMICK, JZ 1984, 65 ff.; see also HAYEK, Constitution, Part II.

27. See FULLER, Morality, Ch. II; see also the criticism SUMMERS, Professor Fuller.

28. RADBRUCH, Rechtsphilosophie § 9.

29. Joseph Raz emphasizes this as the actual basis for the "Rule of Law." RAZ 7.

30. See RAWLS 235 ff.

31. See HENKEL 335, 337. See also GERMANN, Grundlagen 44 ff.; GERMANN, Probleme 28; RADBRUCH, Mensch 96; SCHOLZ 69 ff.

32. See FULLER, Forms, 92 Harvard L. Rev. 372 ff. See also ABA, Rule of Law 28 f.

33. See HALL 27; WIEDEMANN 202. See also KADISH/KADISH 40 ff., 201 ff., who prefer a "checks and balances" model to the more common norm oriented "Rule of Law" model.

34. See RÜMELIN 38 ff.; JESCHECK § 15 III; GERMANN, Rechtssicherheit 62 ff.

35. See KADISH/KADISH 59 ff.; TOMLINSON, 42 Maryland L. Rev. 131, 133, 194 f.

36. RADBRUCH, Rechtsphilosophie 166.

37. GERMANN, Rechtssicherheit 55.

38. See RADBRUCH, Gesetzliches Unrecht, passim.

39. See DWORKIN, Ch. 4 section 3. This paragraph attempts to give expression to Radbruch's antinomies of law for decision of individual cases. See RADBRUCH, Rechtsphilosophie § 9; RADBRUCH, Mensch, Ch. viii.

40. WASSERSTROM 115. See id. 122 f.

41. See WINFIELD, 42 Harvard L. Rev. 76, 92.

42. See Art. 20 III GG; see also MAUNZ/ZIPPELIUS § 12 I; SCHMIDT-BLEIBTREU/KLEIN, Art. 20, margin no. 9; BVerfGE 3, 327.

43. See LEIBHOLZ 287 ff.

44. RADBRUCH, Rechtsphilosophie 165.

45. See the text accompanying notes 47-49 below.

46. RADBRUCH, Mensch 92.

47. See RÜTHERS 119.

48. MAITLAND, Constitutional History 263.

49. See LARENZ 201 f., 410.

50. See FISCHER 32 f.; STEINDORFF, Politik des Gesetzes 235 f.

51. RADBRUCH, Mensch 92 ("Above all, an order which is exclusively in service of the public interest is administration, but never law (*Recht*)"); see also MAITLAND, Constitutional History 263.

52. DWORKIN, Ch. 4.

53. Ibid.

54. HART, American Jurisprudence 141. See STONE 615 ff. Almost a century before the Hart-Dworkin controversy, Oliver Wendell Holmes pointed out the uncertain status of policy in the common law:

> [there is a] paradox of form and substance in the development of law. In form its growth is logical. The official theory is that each new decision follows syllogistically from existing precedents. But . . . precedents survive in the law long after the use they once were is at an end and the reasons for them has been forgotten. . . . On the other hand, in substance the growth of the law is legislative. And this in a deeper sense than that what the courts declare to have always been the law is in fact new. It is legislative in its grounds. The very considerations which judges most rarely mention, and always with an apology, are the secret root from which the law draws all the juices of life. I mean, of course, considerations, of what is expedient for the community concerned. Every important principle which is developed by litigation is in fact and at the bottom the result of more or less definitely understood views of public policy.

HOLMES, Common Law 31 f.

55. See HART, Concept 132.

CHAPTER 3

56. See ENGISCH 106 ff.; LARANZ 276 ff. Compare critical thereto OTT 97 f. The distinction between acts of recognition and value judgments is not the same as the distinction between questions of fact and of law.

57. The synopsis here largely follows that in STEINDORFF, Einführung § 5. Compare STEINDORFF, Zweckmäßigkeit.

58. For "consent decrees," see the text accompanying notes 228 and 246, below.

59. A criticism of this development is PITOFSKY, 127 U. Pennsylvania L. Rev. 1051.

60. Thurman Arnold, probably the best known head of the Antitrust Division wrote:

> prosecution policy in a sense takes in a larger area than judicial policy. It must consider economic factors which cannot be stated in the narrow issues of a case drafted according to the necessary requirement of legal strategy.

ARNOLD, Bottlenecks 186. See Chapter 7 below.

61. Areas not specifically treated below include §§ 2, 3 Clayton Act, which prohibit price discrimination and exclusive dealing, when these lead "substantially to lessen competition or to create a monopoly." Also to be mentioned is § 5 FTC Act.

62. See *National Society of Professional Engineers* v. *United States*, 435 U.S. 679, 688.

63. Ibid. 687.

64. Compare SPENGLER 24 ("so far still no continental jurist has successfully explained or defined the rule of reason completely, let alone even transposed it into German legal concepts").

65. See the text accompanying note 108 below.

66. *Mitchell* v. *Reynolds*, 1 Peere Williams 181, 24 Eng. Rep. 347.

67. See *Standard Oil Co. of New Jersey* v. *United States*, 221 U.S. 1.

68. GELLHORN 176. See *Graphic Products Distributors, Inc.* v. *ITEK Corp.*, 717 F.2d 1560, 1568 n.10.

69. See *National Society of Professional Engineers* v. *United States*, 435 U.S. 679, 691.

70. *Continental T.V. Inc.* v. *GTE Sylvania, Inc.*, 433 U.S. 36, 49.

71. See SULLIVAN 189; see *Graphic Products Distributors, Inc.* v. *ITEK Corp.*, 717 F.2d 1560, 1568 f.; *Marrese* v. *American Academy of Orthopedic Surgeons*, 692 F.2d 1083; *Northwest Power Products, Inc.* v. *Omark Industries, Inc.*, 576 F.2d 83, 90.

72. See BORK, Rule of Reason, 74 Yale L.J. 775, 811 ff.; SULLIVAN § 69.

73. See *National Society of Professional Engineers* v. *United States*, 435 U.S. 679, 692.

74. See *Northern Pacific Railway Co.* v. *United States*, 356 U.S. 1, 5; *Graphic Products Distributors, Inc.* v. *ITEK Corp.*, 717 F.2d 1560, 1566.

75. *Broadcast Music, Inc.* v. *Columbia Broadcasting System, Inc.*, 441 U.S. 1, 9.

76. *National Society of Professional Engineers* v. *United States*, 435 U.S. 679, 692.

77. See for horizontal agreements over prices: *United States* v. *Socony-Vacuum Oil Co.*, 310 U.S. 150; over market division: *United States* v. *Topco Associates*, 405 U.S. 596, 608; over boycotts: *Krol's Inc.* v. *Broadway-Hale Stores, Inc.*, 359 U.S. 207, 212; for vertical agreements establishing price maintenance: *United States* v. *Parke-Davis & Co.*, 362 U.S. 29, 44; over territorial restrictions: *United States* v. *Arnold, Schwinn & Co.*, 388 U.S. 365; see also *Continental T.V. Inc.* v. *GTE Sylvania, Inc.*, 433 U.S. 36 and the text accompanying note 133 below; over tying agreements, see *Jefferson Parish Hospital District No. 2* v. *Hyde*, 466 U.S. 2.

78. OPPENHEIM, 50 Michigan L. Rev. 1139, 1157 f.

79. GELLHORN 178. Further: "Whatever time and effort are required, within tolerable limits, is generally thought to be one of the necessary costs of decency and civilization." Ibid. 178 f.

80. So proceeded the Supreme Court in *Continental T.V. Inc.* v. *GTE Sylvania, Inc.*, 433 U.S. 35.

81. Regarding the creation of "per se rules" the Supreme Court in *Continental T.V. Inc.* v. *GTE Sylvania, Inc.*, said:

> Per se rules thus require the Court to make broad generalizations about the social utility of particular commercial practices. The probability that

> anticompetitive consequences will result from a practice and the severity of those consequences must be balanced against its procompetitive consequences. Cases that do not fit the generalization may arise, but a per se rule reflects the judgment that such cases are not sufficiently common or important to justify the time and expense necessary to identify them. Once established, per se rules tend to provide guidance to the business community and to minimize the burdens on litigants and the judicial system of the more complex rule-of-reason trials, but these advantages are not sufficient in themselves to justify the creation of per se rules. If it were otherwise, all of antitrust law would be reduced to per se rules, thus introducing an unintended and undesirable rigidity in the law.

433 U.S. 36, 50 n.16 (citations omitted).

82. See *United States* v. *Grinnell Corp.*, 384 U.S. 563.

83. See National Commission, Vol. 1, 145 ff.; National Commission Staff Paper, Attempts to Monopolize, 48 Antitrust L.J. 1195.

84. See *United States* v. *Aluminum Co. of America*, 148 F.2d 416.

85. See KAYSEN 340 ff.

86. National Commission, Vol. 1, 160.

87. See SULLIVAN § 203.

88. See Merger Guidelines (1984); Merger Guidelines (1982); Merger Guidelines (1968).

89. See, for example, *Fruehauf Corp.* v. *FTC*, 603 F.2d 345, 353 f.

90. *Ford Motor Co.* v. *United States (Autolite)*, 405 U.S. 562, 570.

91. HAYEK, Counter-Revolution 54.

92. Ibid. 52 f. See also HINTZE, WuW 1970, 571, 578 f.

93. See also MÖSCHEL, Preiskontrollen, JZ 1975, 393, 398.

94. See ST. SEIDENFUS/EWERS 331.

95. See ECKART KOCH, 137 ff.; Att'y Gen. Nat'l Committee 320 ff.

96. See LAMBSDORFF, Geleitwort, WuW 1980, 288, 289.

97. National Commission Vol. 1, 11 f. Compare FIKENTSCHER, Wirtschaftsrecht 365 f.

98. *Brunswick Corp.* v. *Pueblo Bowl-O-Mat, Inc.*, 429 U.S. 477, 488 (emphasis in original); see also *Associated General Contractors* v. *California State Carpenters Council*, 459 U.S. 519.

99. *Broadcast Music, Inc.* v. *Columbia Broadcasting System, Inc.*, 441 U.S. 1, 19.

CHAPTER 4

100. See RADBRUCH, Vorschule 30; see also the text accompanying note 3 above.

101. ENGISCH 107.

102. See KENT *477 ("Lord Mansfield frequently observed, that the certainty of a rule was often of much more importance in mercantile cases than the reason of it . . .").

103. STONE, 22 Modern L. Rev. 597, 599.

104. See LLEWELYN, Bramble Bush 45 ff. For the argument in England respecting determination of the ratio, see GOODHART, Ratio, 22 Modern L. Rev. 117.

105. STONE, 22 Modern L. Rev. 597, 600.

106. LLEWELYN, Präjudizienrecht 79. Further: "In other words, the common law rules do not set boundaries within which one moves. Rather they set guidelines from which one succeeds to the judgment." Ibid.

107. LEVI 1 f., 8 f. See LLEWELYN, Bramble Bush 49.

108. LLEWELYN, Präjudizienrecht 4; LLEWELYN, Rule, 47 Yale L.J. 1243, 1244. See HART, Concept 131.

109. LLEWELYN, Präjudizienrecht 79. More poetically: "the common law rule does not function as a closed space, within which one remains, rather much more as a bough, whose branches are brought forth into growth; in short as a guideline and not as a premise; not as an inflexible suit of armor, which restricts or even rules out growth, but as a skeleton, which supports growth and conditions growth, still promotes and in particular liberates." Ibid. See HART, Concept 132.

110. Departures are above all possible if the case to be decided contains additional fact elements not found in the original precedent (so-called "distinguishing"). See CROSS 25, 187 ff.; LLEWELYN, Bramble Bush 66 ff. Jerome Frank characterized "distinguishing" as "evading or sterilizing" the rule of the precedent, FRANK, Law 159 n.1, or simply as "extinguishing" it. FRANK, Courts 288.

111. See HOLDSWORTH, 50 Law Quarterly Review 180; PLUCKNETT 349 f. See also ALLEN 219 n.1 (who prefers a point later in the nineteenth century); J. H. BAKER 173 f. (who denies the existence of a uniform practice).

112. GOODHART, Precedent, 50 Law Quarterly Rev. 40, 60 f.; see FRANK, Courts 267; SPRECHER, 728 f.

113. See, for example, GRAY 242 f.; KENT *477; *Hertz* v. *Woodman*, 218 U.S. 205, 212.

114. Compare, for example, *Smith* v. *Allwright*, 321 U.S. 649, 665 ("When convinced of former error, this court has never felt constrained to follow precedent."); see LLEWELYN, Common Law Tradition 179 ("Rules are not to control, but to guide decision"), 215 ff.

115. See LEON GREEN 46 ff.; SPRECHER 722 ff.

116. The extent of this freedom is controversial. See *Spector Motor Service* v. *Walsh*, 139 F.2d 809; FRANK, Courts 279 ("Any case is an authoritative precedent only for a judge who, as a result of his own reflection, decides that it is authoritative").

117. See *Bernhardt* v. *Polygraphic Co. of America*, 350 U.S. 198, 205; *Becker* v. *Interstate Properties*, 569 F.2d 1203, 1205 f.; *Cooper* v. *American Airlines, Inc.*, 149 F.2d 355, 359. In this connection it should be recalled that a direct control by the federal courts of the law of the individual states (by appeal) is not possible.

118. See, for example, CARDOZO 113 f. (who also speaks of "gaps" and "open spaces"); HART, American Jurisprudence 128; *Southern Pacific Co.* v. *Jensen*, 244 U.S. 205, 221 (dissenting opinion of Oliver Wendell Holmes). See GOODHART, Precedent, 50 Law Quarterly Rev. 40, 50 (who speaks of "blank spaces").

119. CROSS 34; *Southern Pacific Co.* v. *Jensen*, 244 U.S. 205, 221.

120. See CALABRESI 96 ff. (who speaks of "legal fabric"); COHEN 213 ff.;

FULLER, Anatomy 94 ff.; POUND, Theory, 36 Harvard L. Rev. 940, 952 f.

121. CARDOZO 143.

122. See CARDOZO, Ch. 3; DWORKIN, Ch. 2 §§ 3 f., Ch. 3 § 5; ESSER, Grundsatz, Ch. X; POUND, Justice 56 ff.

123. Amendment vii U.S. CONST.; Fed. R Civ. P. 52(a). See JAMES/HAZARD § 11.3; POUND, Appellate Procedure 4 ff., 221 ff.

124. This review varies, depending upon whether the decision was reached by a judge or jury. A jury decision is to be reversed, only if no reasonable man could have reached their decision, that is, no evidence was produced on which the decision could reasonably be based. See *Galloway* v. *United States*, 319 U.S. 372. A judge's decision is only to be reversed if it is "clearly erroneous." See *Pullman-Standard Division* v. *Swint*, 456 U.S. 273; *Bose Corp.* v. *Consumers Union*, 466 U.S. 485.

125. DAMAŠKA, Structures of Authority, 84 Yale L.J. 480, 515.

126. This classification is often difficult. See *Pullman-Standard Division* v. *Swint*, 456 U.S. 273, 288, 289 n.19.

127. See *Blanton* v. *Mobil Oil Corp.*, 721 F.2d 1207, 1213; see also *Graphic Products Distributors* v. *ITEK Corp.*, 717 F.2d 1560, 1569.

128. 370 U.S. 294 (1962).

129. See, for example, *Fruehauf* v. *United States*, 603 F.2d 345.

130. *United States* v. *American Cyanamid Co.*, 719 F.2d 518.

131. Decisions from other circuits are "persuasive," but not binding. See, for example, *Hasbrouck* v. *Texaco, Inc.*, 663 F.2d 930.

132. In the United States it is generally recognized that despite a 70-year history, the "rule of reason" still is not subject to firm limits. See, for example, *Graphic Products Distributors, Inc.*, v. *ITEK Corp.*, 717 F.2d 1560, 1568. The resulting legal uncertainty is accepted in order to assure that "antitrust liability determinations will turn on the competitive effects of particular conduct rather than simply on broad proscriptive rules." National Commission, Vol. 1, 143.

133. 433 U.S. 36.

134. 388 U.S. 365.

135. 433 U.S. 36, 50. See *Monsanto Co.* v. *Spray-Rite Serivce Corp.*, 465 U.S. 752.

136. See, for example, *Schwegmann Bros.* v. *Calvert Distillers Corp.*, 341 U.S. 384; *Flood* v. *Kuhn*, 407 U.S. 258, 284 f. See AREEDA/TURNER. § 209.

137. See *Parker* v. *Brown*, 317 U.S. 341; *Cantor* v. *Detroit Edison*, 428 U.S. 579; National Commission Staff Paper, State Action, 48 Antitrust L.J. 1281; AREEDA/TURNER §§ 211 ff.

138. See, for example, *Sears, Roebuck & Co.* v. *Stiffel Co.*, 376 U.S. 225.

139. The Supreme Court recently stated: "even when Congress by subsequent legislation establishes a regulatory regime over an area of commercial activity, the antitrust laws will not be displaced unless it appears that the antitrust and regulatory provisions are plainly repugnant." *City of Lafayette* v. *Louisiana Power & Light Co.*, 435 U.S. 389, 398.

140. See generally, OLIPHANT 667 ff.; STONE, 22 Modern L. Rev. 597, 603 ff.

141. See the text accompanying note 121 above.

142. See GRAY 287 ff.; GREENEWALT, 75 Columbia L. Rev. 359, 391 ff.

143. See note 17 above.

144. See GRAY 115, 121 ff.; LLEWELYN, Bramble Bush 42. CROSS, 33 f. ("[The judge] is subject to the even greater restriction that he can only make law on such specific issues as happen to be litigated before him"); FIKENTSCHER, Methoden, Vol. 2, 73.

145. See LLEWELYN, Bramble Bush 42 f., 47.

146. See OLIPHANT 669 ff. For the forms of action system, see MAITLAND, Forms of Action; MAITLAND, Sketch 101 ("He who knows what cases can be brought within each formula knows the law of England. The body of law has a skeleton and that skeleton is the system of writs."); PLUCKNETT 353 ff.

147. The problem of the frivolous lawsuit is chronic in American law and is particularly so in antitrust law, because of its wide-reaching discovery and severe remedies. The cause for this may be found in three circumstances: (1) the right to be heard is especially pronounced in the United States; (2) the parties, not the judge, control the lawsuit; and (3) the parties bear their own attorneys' costs. This problem is often hard for Europeans to understand. In my practice I read the following message from a manager of the American subsidiary of a European firm to his home corporate counsel's office: "According to U.S. law anyone has the right to sue anyone even if there is no legal ground. . . ." Justice Brandeis stated this problem almost as sharply: "Lawsuits often prove to have been groundless; but no way has been discovered of relieving a defendant from the necessity of a trial to establish the fact." *Myers* v. *Bethlehem Shipbuilding Corp*., 303 U.S. 41, 51-52.

148. See *Illinois Brick Co.* v. *Illinois*, 431 U.S. 720.

149. The maxim is: "Equity acts in personam, the law in rem." See CLARK § 15; JAMES/HAZARD § 1.8; SHIPMAN 48.

150. The Sherman Act's system of sanctions is discussed below in Chapter 5.

151. National Commission, Vol. 1, vi.

152. See CALABRESI 1 ff.; FRANKFURTER, 47 Columbia L. Rev. 527.

153. See, for example, GELLHORN 21; HANDLER 3; WYZANSKI 6. Wyzanski is himself a federal judge. His comments illustrate clearly how sharply an American judge's conception of this role can vary from the view his German counterpart has:

> For what irks a trial judge most in this modern statutory, CCH service era is to feel himself operating in a very narrow area where all he can do is define as best he can the words and the purpose of a statute. . . . [I]n such controversies the judge seeks to find, *and not to alter*, the compromise upon which competing interests have elsewhere agreed. But in antitrust matters the trial judge is given again as broad a scope as was enjoyed by the ancient judges who formed the law of tort and those who made the criminal law before the Victorian era. Congress in the widest-sweeping strokes has sketched a grant of almost unlimited authority to the federal courts.

Ibid. (Emphasis in original.) Compare FISCHER 31-32.

154. See CORWIN, 36 Virginia L. Rev. 1.

155. See *McLain* v. *Real Estate Board of New Orleans, Inc.*, 444 U.S. 232; AREEDA/TURNER §§ 231 ff.

156. The crucial concept here is "conscious parallelism," see Att'y Gen. Nat'l Committee 36 ff. Lately the Supreme Court has, however, required "a conscious

commitment to a common scheme designed to achieve an unlawful objective." *Monsanto Co.* v. *Spray-Rite Service Corp.*, 465 U.S. 752.

157. Compare POSNER 214 ff.

158. See EBEL 78 f.; ENGISCH 106 f.; GERMANN, Rechtssicherheit 57; GERMANN, Probleme 281. An analogous conception of the judge's role appeared in the United States in the late nineteenth century and was sharply attacked in the twentieth century as "mechanical jurisprudence," "the phonograph theory," or as formalism. See COHEN 112 ff.; SUMMERS, Instrumentalism 137 ff.

159. Wolfgang Fikentscher (with Kant) and Karl Larenz (with Savigny) begin their historical surveys of German legal methods with the turn of the nineteenth century. See FIKENTSCHER, Methoden, Vol. 3; LARENZ 11. See also DIETZE 46 ff.

160. ENGISCH 107. See also GERMANN, Probleme 282.

161. See RADBRUCH, Gesetzliches Unrecht; ENGISCH 175.

162. BVerfGE 3, 225 f.

163. ENNECCERUS/NIPPERDEY, Vol. 1, § 51 II.

164. LARENZ 160; ENNECCERUS/NIPPERDEY, Vol. 1, §§ 51 ff.; See also SATTELMACHER/SIRP 20.

165. See, for example, BVerfGE 49, 168, 181.

166. ERICHSEN/MARTENS §12 II 1. See also SATTLEMACHER/SIRP 46 ff. Regarding indefinite legal concepts generally, see ENGISCH, 106; the materials cited in notes 167, 168.

167. BACHOF and ULE are the leading proponents of this position. See BACHOF 154; ULE Anwendung.

168. See ERICHSEN/MARTENS § 12 II 1; FORSTHOFF 85 f.; LARENZ 281; ULE, Verwaltungsgerichtsbarkeit § 114 II; ULE, Verwaltungsprozeßrecht § 2 I; WOLFF/BACHOF § 31 I.

169. See ERICHSEN/MARTENS § 12 II 2.

170. See ERICHSEN/MARTENS § 12 II 2; WOLFF/BACHOF § 31 II. BACHOF uses this distinction to mark the division between room for judgment (*Beurteilungsspielraum*) and discretion. See BACHOF 157. See also criticisms: ENGISCH 119 ("It is often only a question of legislative technique, whether discretion concepts are built into the *Tatbestand* or the legal consequence"); H.-J. KOCH 172 f.

171. See WOLFF/BACHOF § 31 II.

172. Ibid.

173. See SOELL 74, 119 ff.; ULE § 2 II.

174. See WOLFF/BACHOF §§ 28 ff., who emphasize:

> Because the judiciary is given independence and is bound only to law, it should be delegated only such questions for decision as can be plainly comprehended and evaluated by a trained jurist relying on his knowledge of life and of the law. As a rule, these are only those questions which arise out of concluded events in the context of a socially prevailing legal system, and not, however, questions whose answers depend on presumptions and estimations of future developments, or which presuppose a change in the prevailing social system (political decisions). As a rule, making decisions which rest on presumptions and which influence the social system are for the politically responsible legislative

> and executive bodies, on whom the administrative bodies must be dependent, because the assumptions and desires of the legislature and executive do not, as facts and statutes do, remain settled objectively. On the other hand, in a *Rechtsstaat* all matters capable of judicial decision should be subject to judicial decision, or at least to judicial review, because this is the best guaranty of objectivity, impartiality, and fairness.

Ibid. § 19 II C. See also LARENZ 119; PICKER. See HART, American Jurisprudence, who emphasizes:

> . . . conventional legal thought in all countries conceives as the standard judicial function: the impartial application of determinate existing rules of law in the settlement of disputes. And what the courts were doing (in America) seems to the English lawyer, at first sight at any rate, particularly hard to justify in a democracy. . . . Certainly a clear-eyed scrutiny of the course of American constitutional decision seems to support the Nightmare view of things and suggests to an Englishman a cynical interpretation of de Tocqueville's observation that political questions in the United States sooner or later become judicial questions. "Perhaps they do so," the Englishman may say, "but the fact that they are decided in American law courts by judges does not mean that they are not there decided politically. So, if your constitution has made law of what elsewhere would be politics, it has done so at the risk of politicising your courts."

Ibid. 125 f.

175. PFEIFFER 5.

176. GÜNTHER, Auslegung 123.

177. See HIRSCH 54 f.; RITTNER, Einführung § 5 B II 1; RITTNER, Rechtssicherheit, WuW 1969, 63. Nevertheless, RITTNER would prefer more legal certainty and less discretion. RITTNER, Ermessen 323 ff. Regarding the importance of Rule of Law security in German law generally, see WIEDEMANN.

178. See IMMENGA in: IMMENGA/MESTMÄCKER § 1 n.32 ff. (who speaks of an "*Abgrenzungsfunktion*"); LANGEN/NIEDERLEITHINGER/SCHMIDT § 1 n.5 (who speak of "*Reichweite*"); RITTNER, Einführung § 6 A I 1a (who speaks of "*begrenzt*").

179. §§ 1, 15, 18, 20, 21, 25. See Ch. 3 above.

180. HIRSCH 54 f.

CHAPTER 5

181. See the text accompanying note 168 above.

182. Uniform specifications in bid solicitation cartels, § 5 IV; export cartels having no domestic operation, § 6 I; uniform standards cartels, § 5 I. See the table in: RINCK § 33.

183. Rationalization by specialization cartels, § 5a; other rationalization cartels for small businesses, § 5b; uniform business terms and discounts cartels, § 2; rebate cartels, § 3.

184. Permission cartels without claim of right: import cartels, § 7; emergency structural crisis cartels, § 4; extraordinary exemption general clause granted by minister of economics, § 8. Permission cartels with claim of right: rationalization cartels, § 5 II; certain rationalization cartels involving agreements on price or on joint procurement or distribution, § 5 III; export cartels having domestic operation.

185. A permission under § 4 has never been granted. See TB 1981/1982, 195. Permissions under § 8 have been only rarely granted. See ibid. vii; RITTNER, Einführung 197 f.

186. See Ch. 7.

187. § 20 III (treating, among other things, patent license agreements) is the only exception, where the possibility of "*Beschränkungen, Bedingungen und Auflagen*" is not expressly anticipated.

188. So-called "*soll*" discretion; see the text accompanying note 171 above. In exceptional cases authorities can grant a longer permission.

189. The only exception is the pure export cartel, which is subject to a special regulation. See § 12 II.

190. Two intervention norms, which concern permissions, allow no or only weak (*soll*) discretion: § 11 V (*muß* provision), § 17 (*soll* provision).

191. Two intervention norms permit positive commands: §§ 11 V, 27. The commands of § 11 might be seen as a belated imposition of conditions, while those of § 27 (permitting the cartel authorities to compel membership in a business association) may be largely motivated by equitable considerations.

192. Another such norm is § 17.

193. See RITTNER, Einführung § 13 D II (who endorses a warning analogous to § 22 V 2).

194. See the text accompanying note 94 above.

195. Nevertheless GERT MEIER expresses Rule of Law criticisms of this intervention norm. See MEIER, WuW 1983, 275. See KARSTEN SCHMIDT, Kartellverfahrensrecht 142 f.

196. See § 823 II BGB.

197. See RINCK § 32 VI 4.

198. See §§ 276, 823 BGB.

199. See GÖHLER/BUDDENDIEK, before § 1(3), page 11.

200. Ibid.

201. TIEDEMANN in: IMMENGA/MESTMÄCKER § 38 n.5

202. Ibid., remark 41 before § 38.

203. See SPENGLER 27. Generally to this problem in German unfair competition law, see KRAFT 235.

204. See RITTNER § 10 D I.

205. See MÖSCHEL, Idee der rule of law, 310 f.; RITTNER, Einführung § 10 D I.

206. See IMMENGA in: IMMENGA/MESTMÄCKER § 1, n.354; THAL, WuW 1970, 319.

207. BGHZ 68, 6, 11 (*Fertigbeton*).

208. See LANGEN/NIEDERLEITHINGER/SCHMIDT, 5th ed., § 1 n.26; RITTNER § 6 A II 3.

209. See LANGEN/NIEDERLEITHINGER/RITTER/SCHMIDT, 6th ed., § 1, n.69 f.

210. See "Deutsche Kooperationsfibel," Zusammenstellung des Bundesministers für Wirtschaft from October 29, 1963, in: BENISCH.

211. Verwaltungsmitteilung des Bundeskartellamtes über die Nichtverfolgung von Kooperationsabreden mit geringer wettbewerbsbeschränkender Bedeutung from July 8, 1980, in: TB 1979/1980, 133 f.

212. See IMMENGA in: IMMENGA/MESTMÄCKER § 1 n.366. See EMMERICH, Kooperation 20 ff.

213. See TB 1981/1982, 7; TB 1979/1980, 7 ff., 134.

214. A declaration of the cartel authorities that there is no basis for action has no effect on the civil law validity of agreements and organizational decisions; see TB 1979/1980, 8. Regarding a change in administration practice, see the text accompanying notes 251-252 below.

215. Fundamentally the cartel authority undertakes departures from the guidelines of July 8, 1980 (above note 211) only in an objective procedure leading to a cease and desist order under § 37a GWB.

216. See KARSTEN SCHMIDT, Zivilrichter, DRiZ 1977, 97, 99.

217. See VELTINS/VELTINS, WRP 1981, 619. For a general assessment of sanctions in German cartel from an American point of view, see HALEY, 59 Washington L. Rev. 471.

218. See the text accompanying note 232 below.

219. See *SCM Corp.* v. *Xerox Corp.*, 463 F. Supp. 983, 999.

220. The National Commission considered and rejected a proposal to eliminate this requirement. See National Commission, Vol. 1, Ch. 8.

221. The activity of the Department of Justice in this area of antitrust law is discussed in Chapter 7.

222. See DONALD BAKER, 63 Cornell L. Rev. 405.

223. For a German view of this procedure ("plea bargaining"), see SCHUMANN.

224. See *Associated General Contractors* v. *California State Carpenters Council*, 459 U.S. 519, 529 ("A literal reading of the statute is broad enough to encompass every injury that can be attributed directly or indirectly to the consequences of an antitrust violation").

225. See, for example, *Brunswick Corp.* v. *Pueblo Bowl-O-Mat, Inc.*, 429 U.S. 477, 485.

226. Ibid. 489. See *J. Truett Payne Co.* v. *Chrysler Motors Corp.*, 451 U.S. 557.

227. See *Associated General Contractors* v. *California State Carpenters Council*, 419 U.S. 519. See also SULLIVAN § 247.

228. KIENAST gives a survey of consent decrees.

229. See MASSEL 98, 138.

230. See *Hartford Empire Co.* v. *United States*, 323 U.S. 386, 409 f.

231. See the text accompanying note 151 above.

232. See the text accompanying note 238 below.

233. See the text accompanying note 218 above.

234. See National Commission, Vol. 1, ch. 7.

235. See the text accompanying note 202 above.

236. See WOLFF/BACHOF § 46.

237. See GRUNSKY § 47 before I; ROSENBERG/SCHWAB § 152 I.

238. For example, if it is once decided in a patent infringement suit that a patent is invalid, then third parties in subsequent cases can rely on this holding. See *Blonder-Tongue Laboratories, Inc.* v. *University of Illinois Foundation*, 402 U.S. 313. If it is once decided in a governmental prosecution that a proxy statement is false and misleading, third parties in subsequent tort cases for fraud can rely on this holding. See *Parklane Hosiery Co.* v. *Shore*, 439 U.S. 322. See also JAMES/HAZARD §§ 11.18 ff.

239. This principal is called "full and fair opportunity to litigate." *Parklane Hosiery Co.* v. *Shore*, 434 U.S. 322, 332. A further limitation may be imposed when the third party could have easily joined as a party in the previous litigation.

240. See GRUNSKY § 47 IV, V, VI; ROSENBERG/SCHWAB §§ 156 f.

241. See the text accompanying notes 243-244 below.

242. BADURA in: ERICHSEN/MARTENS § 41 V; FORSTHOFF § 13; WOLFF/BACHOF § 52. German administrative acts do acquire finality and after a certain period can no longer be challenged; they become *unanfechtbar* and *bestandskräftig*.

243. Decisions of the FTC have no collateral estoppel effect. § 5 Clayton Act after the amendment of Pub. L. 96-349. Decisions of the authorities not to prosecute have no res judicata effect.

244. See § 5 Clayton Act.

245. See, for example, *Marrese* v. *American Academy of Orthopedic Surgeons*, 726 F.2d 1150; *Overseas Motors, Inc.* v. *Import Motors Ltd.*, 375 F. Supp. 499. See H. Rep. No. 96-874, 4 ff.

246. See *United States* v. *Bechtel Corp.*, 648 F.2d 660.

247. Expansion of a consent decree or of an equity decree occurs rarely (if at all). Applications to modify such decrees occur more frequently, see, for example, *United States* v. *American Cyanamid Co.*, 719 F.2d 558, and lately have been more successful than previously. From 1890 to 1967 such modifications to consent decrees were approved only three times where the original adversary did not agree. Note, 80 Harvard L. Rev. 1303, 1311. A consent decree from February 27, 1920 shows that the accomplishment of a modification can be extremely difficult. In 1924, 1928, and 1958 applications for modifications were made, only to be regularly rejected. See *Swift & Co.* v. *United States*, 265 U.S. 311; 286 U.S. 106; 367 U.S. 909. Indeed, in 1969 the government brought suit for conduct in violation of the consent decree. See *United States* v. *Armour & Co.*, 398 U.S. 268. Not until the 1970s was there successful modification and finally, only in 1980, the final dissolution of the consent decree – all only with the acquiescence of the Department of Justice. See *United States* v. *Swift & Co.*, 1971 Trade Cases ¶ 73,760; 1975-1 Trade Cases ¶ 60,201, 1980-1 Trade Cases ¶ 63,185; 1982-1 Trade Cases ¶ 64,464; 1983-1 Trade Cases ¶ 65,250.

248. Recently in another area of law the Supreme Court explicitly recognized the tension between policy decisions and the collateral estoppel doctrine. See *United States* v. *Mendozo*, 464 U.S. 154; see also *Overseas Motors, Inc.* v. *Import Motors Ltd.*, 375 F. Supp. 499, 520 f.; but see also *Nevada* v. *United States*, 463 U.S. 110.

249. See WESTRICK/LÖWENHEIM § 51 margin no. 12; see § 22 VwVfG; STELKENS/BONK/LEONHARDT § 22; WEIDES § 4; WOLFF/BACHOF § 31 II d 1.

250. See BUNTE, 1980 BB 1073.
251. WuW 1981, 541 (*Garant*).
252. WuW 1980, 819, 823 (*Haus und Hofkanalguß*).
253. See ibid.; WuW 1981, 346 (*Schleifscheiben und Schleifkörper*).

CHAPTER 6

254. LEVI 1.

255. See HART, American Jurisprudence 126 ff; SUMMERS, Instrumentalism, Ch. 5,6.

256. See RHEINSTEIN 208. ("The essential difference between common law and civil law lies in the technical structure of court procedure, in the different conceptual framework within which legal thought moves, and in the underlying cause of these differences: the diversity of the personnel by which the machinery of the administration of justice is handled and guided.")

257. See CLARK § 1. The attorney is obliged to instruct the judge in the applicable law. See, for example, *Cicio* v. *City of New York*, 469 N.Y.S.2d 467, 469; Rule 3.3(a)(3) ABA Model Rules; § DR 7-106(B)(I) ABA Model Code.

258. FIKENTSCHER, Methoden, Vol. 2, 71 f.

259. Precedents relate to legal questions, but not to factual determinations. See CROSS 39, 221 ff.

260. Not familiar with the case and not familiar with exactly what the party plans to show, the judge is not well positioned to ask extensive questions. See DAMSAKA, Presentation of Evidence, 123 U. of Pennsylvania L. Rev. 1083, 1090 f.

261. See BORK, Paradox 413 f.; MASSEL 125 f.

262. FULLER, Forms, 92 Harvard L. Rev. 352, 372.

263. RAZ 10.

264. LEVI 5.

265. See DAMASKA, Presentation of Evidence, 123 U. Pennsylvania L. Rev. 1083, 1092; SALTZBURG, 64 Virginia L. Rev. 1, 16 f., 19.

266. It is generally recognized in the United States that the parties to a lawsuit are often not equally well represented, but the only conclusion drawn from this is that the quality of representation should be improved.

267. See the criticisms of two former federal judges: "In short, the lawyer aims at victory, at winning in the fight, not at aiding the court to discover the facts." FRANK, Courts 83; "The key point at every stage . . . is that the single uniformity is always adversariness. There are other goods, but the greatest is winning. There are other evils, but scarcely any worse than losing." FRANKEL 18.

268. Damaska has emphasized:

> It may be in the narrow interest of only one party, or in the common interest of both, that some items of information which the witness possesses do not reach the adjudicator – even though their relevancy in the quest for truth is beyond dispute. Evidence unsupportive of one's case has no function in the adversary litigation process, nor do matters which the parties decide to leave out of the disputation.

DAMASKA, Presentation of Evidence, 123 U. Pennsylvania L. Rev. 1083, 1093. See also ARNOLD, Trial by Combat, 47 Harvard L. Rev. 913.

269. *National Society of Professional Engineers* v. *United States*, 435 U.S. 679, 691 (citing: *Chicago Board of Trade* v. *United States*, 246 U.S. 231, 238).

270. See the text accompanying notes 64-73 above.

271. Ibid. 435 U.S. 679, 692.

272. *Continental T.V. Inc.* v. *GTE Sylvania Inc.*, 433 U.S. 36, 50 n.16.

273. Respecting the simplification, see the criticism, BORK, Paradox 231 ff.

274. See WITHROW/LARMS, 62 Cornell L. Rev. 1. See also MASSEL, Ch. 5 and 6; WESSEL 4 ff. (who calls such cases "socio-scientific").

275. Prettyman Report 64.

276. National Commission, Vol. 1, 324.

277. Ibid. Vol. 2, 116 f.

278. Ibid. Vol. 2, 5.

279. Ibid. Vol. 1, i.

280. Ibid. iii. See BAYLSON, 48 Antitrust L.J. 705; National Commission Staff Paper, Early Narrowing of Issues, 48 Antitrust L.J. 1041; National Commission Staff Paper, Scope of Discovery, 48 Antitrust L.J. 1063. See also *Marrese* v. *American Academy of Orthopedic Surgeons*, 692 F.2d 1083, 706 F.2d 1488, 726 F.2d 1150.

281. National Commission, Vol. 1, 63.

282. Ibid. Vol. 1, 12.

283. Ibid. Vol. 1, 17. See National Commission Staff Paper, Expediting Complex Antitrust Cases, 48 Antitrust L.J. 1121.

284. Some judges expressed concern that a "special roster" might lead to "elitism." National Commission, Vol. 1, 21.

285. See SALTZBURG, 64 Virginia L. Rev. 1, 81. See the text accompanying note 146 above.

286. See the text accompanying note 261 above.

287. See the text accompanying note 146 above.

288. See RESNIK, 96 Harvard L. Rev. 376.

289. See JAUERNIG § 25 I; ROSENBERG/SCHWAB § 78 II.

290. See GRUNSKY § 3.

291. See JAUERNIG § 25 V; SATTELMACHER/SIRP 71 ff., 75 ff. In part the *Schlüßigkeitsprüfung* resembles the demurrer of the common law (see JAMES/HAZARD §§ 4.1 f.); however the demurrer presupposes application of a party.

292. See DAMAŠKA, Presentation of Evidence, 123 U. Pennsylvania L. Rev. 1083, 1087; LARENZ 197.

293. See GRUNSKY §§ 3, 18; ROSENBERG/SCHWAB §§ 78 f.; E. SCHMIDT, margin no. 355 ff.

294. See GRUNSKY § 19.

245. See ibid.

296. See DAMAŠKA, Presentation of Evidence, 123 U. Pennsylvania L. Rev. 1083, 1088 f.

297. See the criticism of cartel law in LIEBERKNECHT 70 ff.

298. See Ch. 7 below.

299. See GRÜTZNER; HERMANNS; WECKMANN.

300. See § 28 I VwVfG; see also GRIESSHABER; HERTIN.

301. GÜNTHER, Auslegung 127.

302. PFEIFFER 11.

303. GÜNTHER, Auslegung 124 (emphasis in original); see also STEINDORFF, Politik des Gesetzes 230.

304. Ibid. 125 f. (emphasis in original).

305. See the text accompanying note 167 above.

CHAPTER 7

306. Such a view of *all* law has appeared in the United States. Robert Summers has dubbed it "robust predictivism." SUMMERS, Instrumentalism, Ch. 5.

307. See BegrGWB, Part B, III ff.; See WEBER, Vol. 2, 569 ff. (pp. 973 ff. in the translation).

308. FULLER, Adversary System 44. See ABA Model Code, § EC 7-19.

309. For example, from 1958 to 1984, some 604 registrations of cartels or applications for permissions were filed with the Federal Cartel Authority, but only 153 with all the provincial authorities combined. TB 1983/1984, 140 ff.

310. See, for example, Bay Kartellbericht 1978/1979, 28 ff.

311. See Art. 83, 84 III GG.

312. BROSE/HELMCKE, WuW 1981, 845, 846.

313. See ibid. 847; RITTNER, Ermessen 314 f.

314. See, for example, ibid. 848 ff. The Department of Justice has announced a similar policy, limited, however, to questions of law. See SMITH.

315. WERNER SCHNEIDER provides a somewhat outdated overview of the Federal Cartel Authority.

316. See KLAUE in: IMMENGA/MESTMÄCKER § 48, n.2. Regarding the positions of higher federal agencies, see THIEME § 42.

317. See RITTNER, Einführung § 14 B II 2.

318. KLAUE in: IMMENGA/MESTMÄCKER § 48 n.8.

319. Ibid. n.5.

320. LANGEN/NIEDERLEITHINGER/RITTER/SCHMIDT, 6th ed., § 48 n.6.

321. See THOMAS RAISER, BB 1972, 471.

322. See § 48 II 1.

323. See ZUCK, Wirtschaftspolitik, NJW 1971, 1633, 1635; see also ZUCK, Bundeswirtschaftsministerium; BB 1973, 20, 23.

324. KLAUE in: IMMENGA/MESTMÄCKER § 48 n.11.

325. See KARTTE 55.

326. See KLAUE in: IMMENGA/MESTMÄCKER § 48 n.12 ff.

327. "Über die Anwendung des § 22 GWB auf abgestimmte Verhaltensweisen," (BAnz No. 107, June 15, 1971); "über die Intensivierung der Mißbrauchsaufsicht über vertikale Preisbindungen und -empfehlungen" (BAnz No. 231, November 30, 1973); "über Zusagen in Zusammenschlußkontrollverfahren" (BAnz No. 66, April 3, 1976); "über die Aufstellung von Leitsätzen zur leistungssteigernden Kooperation" (BAnz No. 46, March 7, 1978); "über die Behandlung von Auslandszusammenschlüssen" (BAnz No. 103, June 7, 1980). Cited following LANGEN/NIEDERLEITHINGER/RITTER/SCHMIDT, 6th ed. § 49 n.2.

328. See KLAUE in: IMMENGA/MESTMÄCKER § 49 n.1.

329. See KLAUE in: IMMENGA/MESTMÄCKER § 49 n.5 f.
330. See KLAUE in: IMMENGA/MESTMÄCKER § 49 n.2.
331. See KARTTE 55.
332. See RITTNER, Einführung § 8 D V.
333. BegrGWB Part B, III ff.
334. Ibid.
335. Ibid.
336. See DAMASKA, Structures of Authority, 84 Yale L.J. 480, 489 f.
337. PFEIFFER 3.
338. ROSENBERG/SCHWAB § 135 I. Although this right has over time been limited, most recently by amendment in 1976, it remains considerable, particularly in comparison to American appeals; see §§ 525, 528 ZPO.
339. See §§ 525, 537 ZPO.
340. See §§ 538 ff. ZPO.
341. See § 66 OWiG.
342. See GÖHLER/BUDDENDIEK, vor § 67, n.2 (*Beschuldigung*).
343. See STEINDORFF, Möglichkeiten, ZHR, Vol. 174, 520, 524 (who considers the review given decisions not to prosecute insufficient).
344. See § 46 III 3 OWiG. See also ZUCK, Dienstaufsicht, NJW 1972, 468.
345. See § 86 I VwGO.
346. See § 42 I VwGO.
347. See § 42 II Vw GO.
348. See LANGEN/NIEDERLEITHINGER/SCHMIDT, 5th ed., § 62 n.10.
349. Turning down requested administrative order might be an overstepping of discretion. See ERICHSEN/MARTENS § 12 II 2 b cc; MÜLLER/GRIES § 62 n.4.
350. See § 114 VwGO.
351. See § 70 V.
352. Even the opponents of this point of view concede it to be dominant; see LANGEN/NIEDERLEITHINGER/SCHMIDT, 5th ed., § 70 n.16 f. It is said that § 70 V 1 may be explained by a failure to distinguish adequately between what is now discussed as room for judgment (*Beurteilungsspielraum*) of the *Tatbestand* and discretion for action (*Handlungsermessen*) in the choice of legal consequence. The legislature wanted to assure full review of whatever room for judgment the many indefinite legal concepts might give the cartel authorities; see BENKENDORFF, Rechtskontrolle, WuW 1958, 740; GEORGE; HALBEY, WRP 1968, 349, 351; RINCK § 41, margin no. 1061; WÜRDINGER.
353. WESTRICK/LÖWENHEIM § 70 n.27 ("compensation for the legal uncertainty of the *Tatbestände* of cartel law norms").
354. HALBEY, WRP 1968, 350. Denying the cartel authorities the power of decision was felt would make it too difficult for enforcement of the law to keep up with the dynamic of the economy. Ibid.
355. See LANGEN/NIEDERLEITHINGER/SCHMIDT, 5th ed., § 70 n.17.
356. See BegrGWB Part B, V.
357. See the text accompanying notes 377-393 below.
358. KATZMANN provides an overview of the FTC.
359. For a German view of U.S. prosecutors, see WEIGEND, Ch. 6.
360. See the text accompanying note 388 below.

361. Massel came to this conclusion prior to the criticism of the 1960s. See MASSEL 124.

362. Amendment vii U.S. Const.

363. Rule 38, Fed. R. Civ. P. In contrast, in criminal cases the accused must explicitly abandon his right to jury trial. Rule 31, Fed. R. Crim. P.

364. See JORDE, 69 California L. Rev. 1; SPERLICH, 65 Judicature 394.

365. See LLEWELYN, Präjudizienrecht 36; SALTZBURG, 64 Virginia L. Rev. 1, 22 ff.

366. Vaughn 135, 124 Eng. Rep. 1006. See KADISH/KADISH 45 ff.; THOMPSON, Vol. 1, vi, Ch. 29, Vol. 2, Ch. 60.

367. See the text to note 372 below.

368. See Rule 50, Fed. R. Civ. P.; *Graphic Products Distributors, Inc.* v. *ITEK Corp.*, 717 F.2d 1560, 1566.

369. See NORDENBERG/LUNEBURG, 65 Judicature 420. In one antitrust case the foreman of the jury said: "If you can find a jury that's both a computer technician, a lawyer, an economist, knows all that stuff, yes, I think you could have a qualified jury, but we don't know anything about that." *H.C. Peripherals Leasing Corp. (Memorex)* v. *IBM Corp.*, 458 F. Supp. 423, 448. See SPERLICH, 65 Judicature 394, 405. This criticism of the jury is new only with respect to complex cases. See THOMPSON, Vol. 1, v. ("The jury which really tries the case is often composed of the most ignorant men who can be found in the community.")

370. See Rule 49, Fed. R. Civ. P.

371. Because of the general verdict Jerome Frank said: "a better instrument than the usual jury trial could scarcely be imagined for achieving uncertainty, capriciousness, lack of uniformity, disregard of the [rules], and unpredictability of decisions." FRANK, Law 186.

372. See *Zenith Radio Corp.* v. *Matsushita Elec. Indus. Co.*, 478 F. Supp. 889, 938 ("Thus when justice requires, juries can reach results at variance with the law"); FRANK, Courts 127 ff.; SPERLICH, 65 Judicature 394, 414; STEPHEN 208.

373. LLEWELYN, Präjudizienrecht 29.

374. *Jones* v. *Barnes*, 463 U.S. 745.

375. DAMAŠKA, Structures of Authority, 84 Yale L.J. 480, 515. Regarding American appellate procedure, see KARLEN; LLEWELYN, Common Law Tradition; POUND, Appellate Procedure.

376. See generally WEIGEND 94, 98 ff., 108 ff.

377. The defendant has a limited constitutional right to learn what evidence the prosecutor has developed against him. See *Brady* v. *Maryland*, 373 U.S. 83; see also SCHLESINGER, 26 Buffalo L. Rev. 361, 372 ff.

378. Cited after HOLSENDOLPH. The trial court is reported to have given some resistance to this step, apparently looking to the new statute regulating consent decrees. See the article "When judges object to antitrust dismissals," in: Business Week, April 19, 1982, 27.

379. DAVIS, Discretionary Justice 192.

380. Ibid. 192 f.

381. See DAMAŠKA, Structures of Authority, 84 Yale L.J. 480 (who provides a different explanation).

382. See also HAZARD 131.

383. See MARK GREEN et al. 82 ff.; WEAVER 131.

384. SULLIVAN § 127.

385. § 2 Pub. L. 93-528.

386. *United States* v. *Bechtel Corp.*, 648 F.2d 660, 666 (citations omitted).

387. The proposal of Walton Hamilton and Irene Till may be the only one of this type to have obtained an audience. See HAMILTON/TILL.

388. See, for example, National Commission, Vol. 1, 365 ff. (dissenting opinion of Commissioner Senator Orrin Hatch and Congressman Charles Wiggins); ABA FTC Commission Report 97 f. (dissenting opinion of commissioner, now federal judge, Richard Posner); WHITE, 61 A.B.A.J. 1242.

389. See WEAVER 175.

390. SHENEFIELD.

391. See note 314 above.

392. See SHENEFIELD 20 ff.; WEAVER Ch. 4 and 5.

393. POSNER 231.

CHAPTER 8

394. See BORK, Ch. 22.

395. ESSER, Note 168.

396. See PICKER, JZ 1984, 153, 155 ff.

Index

About the Author

JAMES R. MAXEINER practices law in New York City on behalf of an international clientele primarily in the fields of trade regulation and litigation. Before entering private practice, Dr. Maxeiner served as an attorney with the evaluation section of the Antitrust Division of the U.S. Department of Justice.

Dr. Maxeiner is educated in common and in civil law systems. He holds a J.D. with Specialization in International Legal Affairs from Cornell University, an LL.M. (in international and comparative law) from Georgetown University, and a Dr. Jur. from the University of Munich. His undergraduate degree in history is from Carleton College. His publications in comparative law and in legal history have appeared in the United States and in Europe.